Home Automation & Security Proj[ects]

for Raspberry Pi (Book 2)

Tim Rustige

Home Automation & Security Projects for Raspberry Pi (Book 2)

© Tim Rustige

First published: May 2017

Published by TR Computers Limited.

All Trademarks & Registered Trademarks are hereby acknowledged.

Raspberry Pi and the Raspberry Pi logo are registered trademarks of the Raspberry Pi Foundation.

All rights reserved. No part of this book or any of the software featured may be reproduced or translated in any form without the prior written consent of the author.

Disclaimer: Whilst every effort has been made to ensure all the information contained in this book is accurate, the author & publisher can accept no liability for any consequential loss or damage, however caused, arising as a result of using the information contained.

All the projects in this book are also available as complete projects kits from:

www.trcomputers.co.uk

http://stores.ebay.co.uk/convertstuffuk

https://www.amazon.co.uk/s?merchant=A3FJQLQ9748AAR&fallThrough=1

Table of Contents

Introduction..5

Connect a Wireless Doorbell to your Pi..8
Wireless doorbell & PIR receiver project..9
Connecting to an older Raspberry Pi model A or B...10
Connecting to a Raspberry Pi B+, A+, Pi Zero, Pi 2 or Pi 3..11
Install WiringPi library...12
 Install 433Utils..12
Photo of test.sh script & the output it produces:..14
A word about the way folders & files are organised on a Raspberry Pi........................15
How to make an executable script..16
Setting up a spare Gmail account, just for your Pi to use..17
Setup the Raspberry Pi camera module...20
Text overlay date & time on a photo...22
How to attach a buzzer to the Raspberry Pi...24
How to play an MP3 file when the doorbell is pressed..26
How to connect your Pi to your WiFi router using a USB WiFi dongle.........................27
How to make your Pi automatically run our scripts at startup.......................................28
Night & day photo emailer script for PiNoIR camera...29
A script that detects a doorbell & a PIR sensor..30
Using a Sony PS2 or PS3 Eye Toy USB webcam to take photos.................................31
Script to grab photo from webcam when door is opened...32
Script to capture photos from Easycap USB video grabber..33
Bluetooth scanning..34
Set up Wifi Sniffing on Raspbian build...35
Scan for WiFi Probe Requests...35
Connect to your Pi remotely from your PC..37
How to transfer files from your Pi to PC using Filezilla..38

Reverse Engineering Wireless Gadgets..39
How to receive codes from a wireless remote on your Raspberry Pi...........................40
Transmitting signals..44
Remote control mains sockets...47
Replaying a captured code...53
Remote control mains relays..55
How to connect the relay to an LED panel and 12 volt battery pack............................56
How to connect the relay to other voltages...57

How to control hardware from a web browser interface..59
Connect an LED to GPIO pin 4 and control it from a web browser..............................60
Install WiringPi library...61
Install Apache Web Server...62
Setup the CGI scripts to make the web page buttons active..64
Setup port forwarding on your router...65
Controlling Wireless Mains Sockets from a web browser...66
Using a PHP web page to control an LED..69
Using a PHP web page to remote control main sockets...71

How to stream CCTV audio over a network..74
Audio capture hardware options...75

- A CCTV microphone..75
- Power supply for the CCTV Mic...76
- USB Audio line-level capture device..76
- Streaming Audio from one Raspberry Pi to another...77
- On the receiving Pi...78
- On the sending Pi:...79
- Audio Mixer Panel..80
- Different audio sampling rates...81

Pan and tilt camera controller...82
- Pan & tilt camera bracket for Raspberry Pi..83
- Wiring Diagram..84
- Servo Driver Software..86
- Desktop control panel to pan & tilt...87
- SSH remote pan & tilt with streaming to VLC..87
- Installing the web browser camera control applications..88
- Streaming video to a web browser...89

Introduction

In our first Home Security Projects book for Raspberry Pi we showed you how to connect PIR motion sensors and magnetic door/window sensors to your Pi, and have your Pi email photos to your mobile phone when activity was detected.

In this second book we build on that by showing you how to connect a cheap wireless doorbell to the internet, and get photos of callers emailed to your phone. We also show you how to create your own home automation system, using inexpensive wireless mains sockets, light switches & relays, and control them from your tablet or mobile phone's web browser - you can also have the Pi turn the appliances on and off at pre-set times.

In later chapters we show you how to make a motorised cctv security camera that you can pan & tilt from a web browser on your phone, and also control from a graphical panel on your Pi's desktop.

If you've ever wondered how to stream CCTV audio from one Pi to another over a network or the internet, we also show you the best USB Audio capture and microphone hardware to use and the simplest way to stream it from the command line.

All our wireless projects use the licence-free 315MHz equipment in North America and 433.92MHz in the UK/Europe. The typical equipment that operates at these frequencies is very inexpensive.

Here are some examples of typical costs on eBay:

433MHz super heterodyne shielded wireless receiver module 30 metre range - £4/$5

433MHz transmitter & receiver boards for Arduino/Raspberry Pi - £2/$3

3 Pack of Status Remote Control Mains sockets 433MHz - £15/$19

Remote control light switches 1,2 or 3 gang - £12/$15

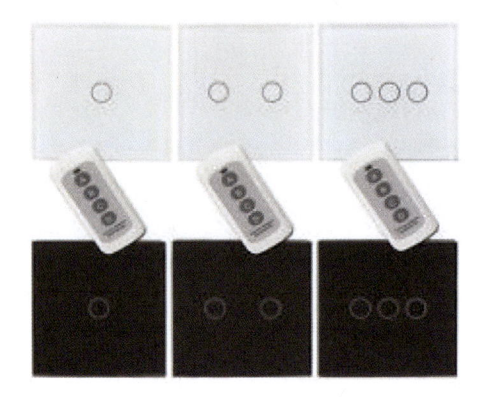

433MHz 12 volt relays – use to control 5 or 12 volt DC or 240/120V AC mains 10A - £3/$4

433MHz Lloytron MIP wireless Doorbell push available in White or Black - £5/$6

433MHz Lloytron MIP wireless PIR motion sensor - £11/$14

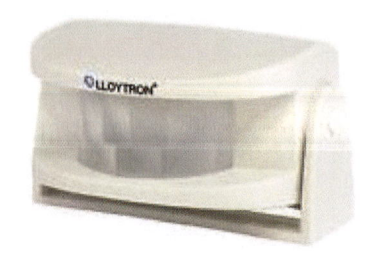

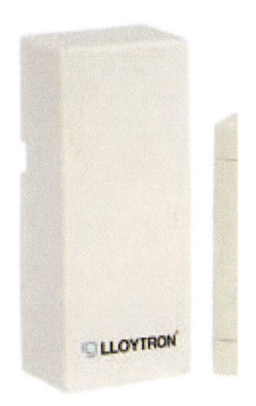

433MHz Lloytron MIP wireless door sensor - £6/$8

Using the standard 433MHz receiver and transmitter boards, it's possible to "talk & listen" to a wide range of equipment using any model of Raspberry Pi – you're not locked into a single manufacturer, like you would be if you'd bought Energenie power sockets and installed their wireless GPIO hat.

The scripts in subsequent chapters show you how to receive codes and timing values from your 433MHz or 315MHz wireless devices, and then be able to replay those codes from simple Python scripts running on your Pi.

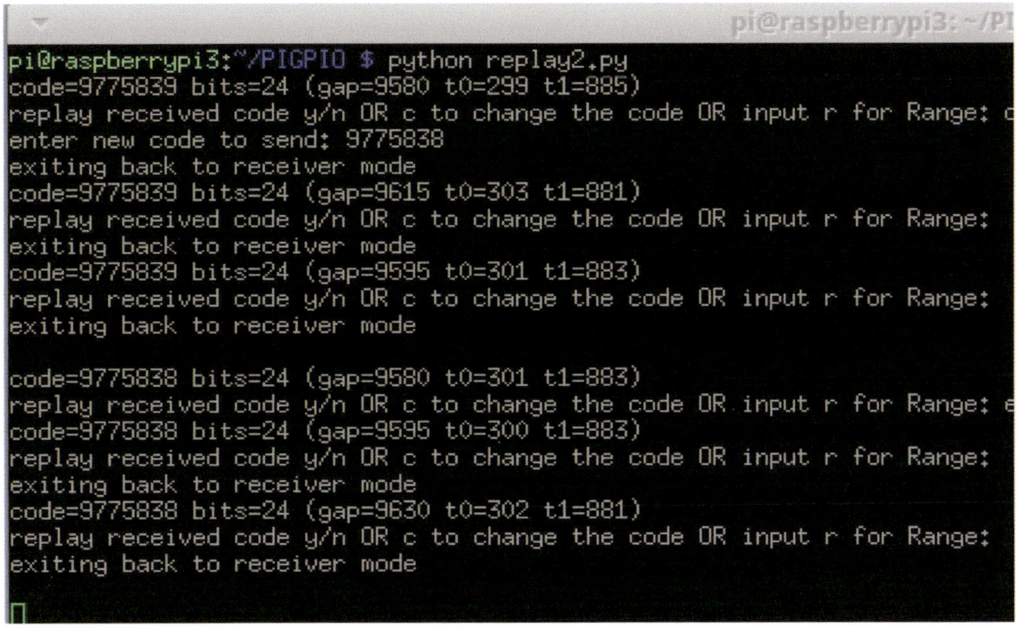

We show you how to transmit codes to turn mains sockets, relays & light switches on and off at certain times of day. We also show you how to create a web browser interface that lets you control mains sockets, relays and light switches from your phone or tablet over WiFi or the internet.

Say goodbye to manually trying to reverse-engineer 433MHz and 315MHz OOK AM signals using Audacity, Baudline, GNUradio, Inspectrum etc.

Connect a Wireless Doorbell to your Pi.

Wireless doorbell & PIR receiver project.

This project will allow your Raspberry Pi to listen out for the 433MHz radio signal transmitted by a variety of Lloytron MIP wireless doorbells, PIR sensors & Magnetic door sensors. It will also detect signals from Driveway Patrol & Digiteck driveway alarms.

The Pi can differentiate between the unique codes from each device & send you an email stating which has been triggered. If you have a Raspberry Pi camera or USB webcam pointing at the doorway, you can get a photo of the visitor emailed to your mobile phone.

You'll need: 433MHz receiver board , mini breadboard, three IDC connection wires (all pictured), 5 volt buzzer & 2 connection wires.

Connecting to an older Raspberry Pi model A or B

The blue wire in the picture is an optional antenna wire, which should be 17.3cm long & can be coiled around a biro so it takes up less space. We didn't need to use an external antenna wire in any of our tests.

The colour of the wires isn't important, just make sure connect the correct points together.

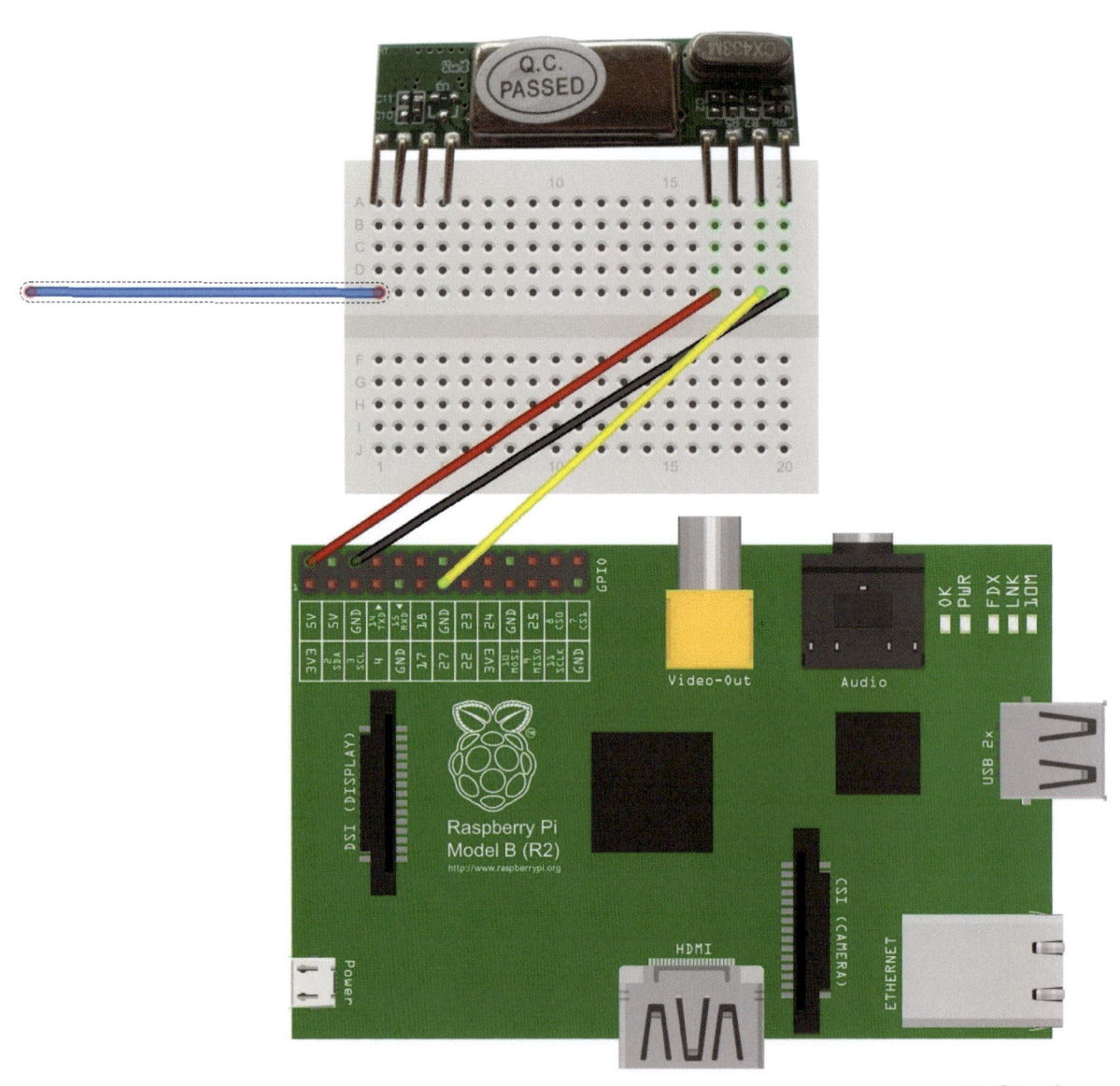

Connecting to a Raspberry Pi B+, A+, Pi Zero, Pi 2 or Pi 3.

The blue wire in the picture is an optional antenna wire, which should be 17.3cm long & can be coiled around a biro so it takes up less space. We didn't need to use the external antenna wire in any of our tests.

You can use different coloured wires, just make sure you connect the correct points together.

The red wire connects to 5 volt + on the Pi, the black wire connects to GND & the yellow wire connects to GPIO 27 (which in WiringPi-speak is confusingly referred to as GPIO 2)

11

Install WiringPi library

Before we go any further we need to install WiringPi, a set of utilities that make talking to the GPIO pins easy. Enter these commands at the $ terminal prompt:

```
sudo apt-get update
sudo apt-get upgrade
sudo apt-get install git-core
git clone git://git.drogon.net/wiringPi
```

```
cd wiringPi
git pull origin
```

```
./build
gpio -v
gpio readall
cd ..
```

You'll now see a list of all the GPIO assignments for Wiring Pi. I've highlighted our GPIO pin 27.

Install 433Utils

Install 433Utils

Next, we need to install a set of 433Mhz radio utilities written in the C programming language. We use C for this part, because Python or a shell script are too slow. When entering the commands below, remember that Linux & the Raspberry Pi are case-sensitive, so 433Utils isn't the same as 433utils.

```
git clone --recursive git://github.com/ninjablocks/433Utils.git
cd 433Utils/RPi_utils
```

With the utils installed, we now need to patch them with some code from our website, so we can make RFSniffer interact with our shell scripts. First move the RFSniffer.cpp source code to a different filename & then download our 433.zip file. Finally compile everything with Make.

```
mv RFSniffer.cpp oldRFSniffer.cpp
wget http://www.securipi.co.uk/433.zip
tar xvf 433.zip
chmod a+x *.sh
make
ls -al
```

You should now see a list of files. The test.sh file will let you figure out the codes being sent by your various Lloytron devices and driveway alarms.

```
sudo ./test.sh
```

Now press your doorbell or activate your PIR. If the code being transmitted matches the valid string in the test.sh file, then you get a good read message and the numeric code of your device is displayed, but if the code doesn't match you get a BAD READ message, and the numeric code received is displayed.

Write down the numerical codes for each of your devices on a piece a paper for use later on. You can stop the test.sh script from running by holding down Ctrl-C on the keyboard. You can edit the test.sh script, so it says your doorbell or PIR is valid like this:

```
nano test.sh
```

look for the line that says valid="457624" & change the number to your code.

Ctrl-O + Enter to save the file & then Ctrl-X to exit. Now run the test.sh file again

```
sudo ./test.sh
```

Now, when the doorbell or PIR is activated, you should see your code as the valid one.

Ctrl-C to quit the test.sh script.

Photo of test.sh script & the output it produces:

1. Lloytron Doorbell 1   457624 (current valid code)
2. Lloytron Doorbell 2   16644136
3. Lloytron Magnetic door sensor   5301448
4. Lloytron PIR movement detector   8699400

Each of our Lloytron devices always send the same code. Your devices will have different codes.

```
root@raspberrypi:/home/pi/433Utils/RPi_utils# cat test.sh
while true;  do
        valid="457624"
        scan=`./RFSniffer`
                if [ "$scan" == "$valid" ]; then
                        echo "Good Read"
                        echo "Your code is " $scan
                else
                        echo "BAD READ:  your code and the valid don't match"
                        echo "Your correct valid code should be " $scan
                fi
        sleep 5
done
exit
root@raspberrypi:/home/pi/433Utils/RPi_utils#
root@raspberrypi:/home/pi/433Utils/RPi_utils#
root@raspberrypi:/home/pi/433Utils/RPi_utils# ./test.sh
Good Read
Your code is  457624
BAD READ:  your code and the valid don't match
Your correct valid code should be  16644136
BAD READ:  your code and the valid don't match
Your correct valid code should be  5301448
BAD READ:  your code and the valid don't match
Your correct valid code should be  5301448
BAD READ:  your code and the valid don't match
Your correct valid code should be  8699400
Good Read
Your code is  457624
Good Read
Your code is  457624
```

If you don't have the Lloytron wireless MIP doorbells & sensors, but a different make or model and don't see a code displayed, then your doorbell or PIR isn't compatible with 433Utils, sorry.

If you do have the Lloytron MIP sensors and aren't seeing a code produced, then it's likely the receiver module is wired incorrectly or your doorbell/PIR isn't close enough to the Pi (initially test everything in the same room, within 2 metres).

A word about the way folders & files are organised on a Raspberry Pi.

If you've just ran the ./test.sh file on the previous page and decide to power off & come back to your Raspberry Pi tomorrow, you'll notice that when the Pi next powers up you won't be able to find the test.sh file again easily. This is because we installed it into the folder /home/pi/433Utils/RPi_utils.

So next time you power up your Pi, & login in as user Pi, do this:

```
cd ~/433Utils/RPi_utils
ls -al
```

and you'll see the list of files for this project.

Type in

```
cd ..
```

and you'll move up one folder level to folder /home/pi/433Utils

type in `cd ..` again and you'll be in folder /home/pi

to print the current working directory, type in

```
pwd
```

If you want to make your Pi always go into folder /home/pi/433Utils/RPi_utils on bootup, type in

```
nano /home/pi/.profile
```

make the last line say

```
cd ~/433Utils/RPi_utils
```

Ctrl-O to WriteOut and then Ctrl-X to Exit

When you reboot your Pi you should automatically go to folder /home/pi/433Utils/RPi_utils.

How to make an executable script.

We've assumed you're running the latest version of the Raspbian OS for the Raspberry Pi. (There's an ISO image of it on the DVD and instructions for making a bootable SD card at the end of this document).

When you see us change font to `courier`, we are indicating a command you type into the command line. For example:

```
nano test2.sh
```

Will open a basic text editor & allow you to enter a series of commands, that form the basis of all our scripts. Enter the following text:

```
echo "hello world"
```

Then save the file & exit. To make the command executable type:

```
chmod u+x test2.sh
```

and then to run the script

```
./test2.sh
```

Some scripts will need to be run as root (the highest security level). To do that type:

```
sudo ./test2.sh
```

To see a list of files in the current folder type

```
ls -al
```

If you have any problem running a script, then you've either made a typo, forgotten to make it executable with `chmod`, or need to put a `sudo` in front of it.

If you get bored of entering `sudo` before each command, you can switch to root by entering:

```
sudo su
```

You'll notice the prompt then changes from $ to #. You can exit root by pressing Ctrl-D. While you're in root mode it's a good idea to change the default passwords for root & user pi, like this:

```
passwd
passwd pi
```

Setting up a spare Gmail account, just for your Pi to use.

The simplest way of sending emails & photos as attachments from your Pi, is to setup a new Gmail account for the Pi to use, even if you already have an existing Gmail account you use on your phone or PC. For one thing, it gets you 15GB of new cloud storage for your alert photos & secondly it removes the complication of generating application specific passwords for other apps on your existing Gmail account.

You need to create the new Gmail account in the web browser on your PC or Mac @

https://accounts.google.com/SignUp?service=mail

and note down the login & password for later. Don't use the # symbol in your password as it causes the Pi problems. Lower & upper-case letters & number combinations are always fine though.

Next, you need to set the new Gmail account to Enable "less secure apps". While logged in go to:

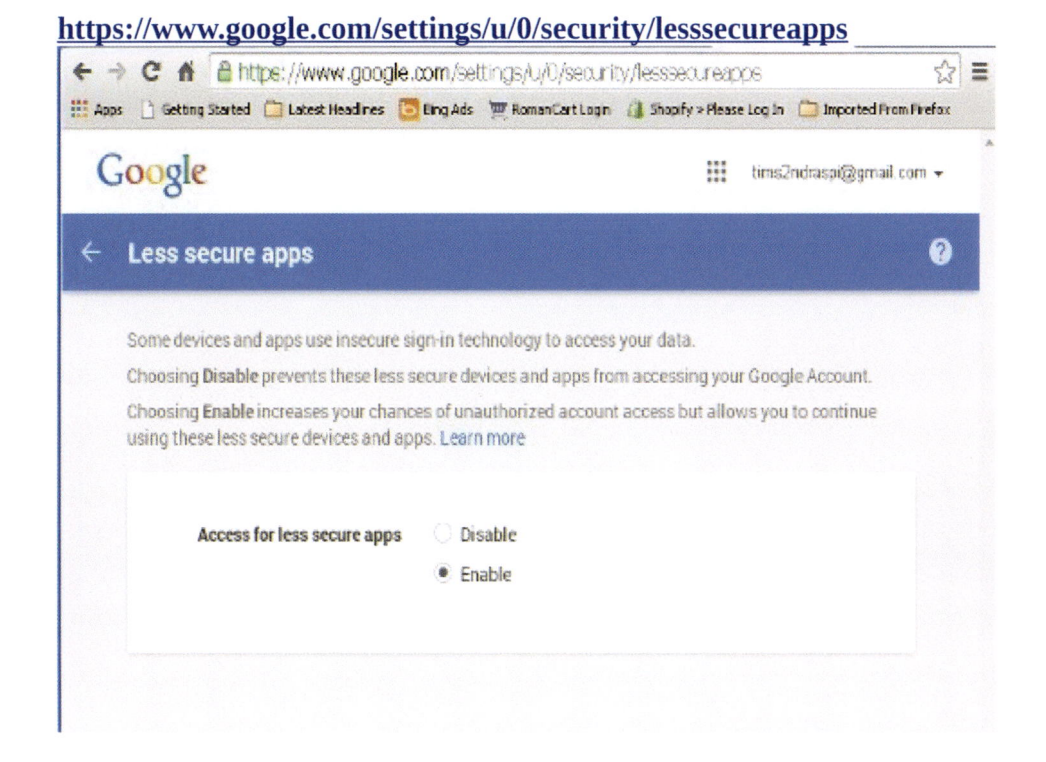

https://www.google.com/settings/u/0/security/lesssecureapps

Now we have a working email account, just for the Pi to use when sending emails. Any photos sent from the Pi will be backed-up in the Sent folder & you only need delete old photos if you get near to the 15GB limit. Emails from the Pi can be sent to any other email address on your phone or PC.

17

Send an email when the doorbell or PIR is triggered

This script builds on test.sh by adding basic email capability & event logging to a text file.

```
nano alarm1.sh
```

Then enter the following commands into the nano editor:

```sh
#!/bin/sh
while true;  do
        valid="457624"
        scan=`./RFSniffer`
                if [ "$scan" = "$valid" ]; then
                        d=`date +%d%m%y`
                        t=`date +%T`
                        echo "Alarm triggered $t $d" | mail -s "Alarm" youremailaddress@gmail.com
                        echo "Alarm triggered $t $d"
                        echo "Alarm triggered $t" >> log$d.txt

                else
                        echo "bad read your code and valid dont match"
                        echo $scan
                fi
        sleep 20
done
exit 0
```

Save the file & exit.

Once again, make the script executable with

```
chmod u+x alarm1.sh
```

Before we can run the script we need to install & configure several mail applications from the internet. You also need to have made a new Gmail account, just for the Pi to use and enable "less secure app" access @ https://www.google.com/settings/u/0/security/lesssecureapps

```
sudo apt-get install ssmtp
sudo apt-get install mailutils
sudo apt-get install mpack
```

Setup default settings SSMTP.

```
sudo nano /etc/ssmtp/ssmtp.conf
```

```
AuthUser=your-gmail-account@gmail.com
AuthPass=your-user-password
FromLineOverride=YES
mailhub=smtp.gmail.com:587
UseSTARTTLS=YES
```

save file & exit.

Send a test email with this command, substituting the email address below with your own.

```
echo "testing 1 2 3" | mail -s "Subject" you@yourdomain.co.uk
```

Assuming that worked okay, you can now run the alarm1.sh script.

```
sudo ./alarm1.sh
```

When the drive alarm is triggered you should see "Alarm Triggered" appear on the display, a record will also be added to the date stamped text file. Now check your emails & you should have a record of the alarm being triggered. You can quit the alarm1.sh script with Ctrl-C.

You can check the contents of a time stamped log file with:

```
cat log060613.txt
```

You can see a list of all your log files with:

```
ls -al log*.txt
```

If you have lots of entries in your log file, you can pause the display with:

```
cat log060613.txt | more
```

or you can open the file in the editor with:

```
nano log060613.txt
```

If you notice the time & date aren't set correctly, you can run:

```
sudo dpkg-reconfigure tzdata
```

Setup the Raspberry Pi camera module.

Install latest version of Raspbian to an SD card.

```
sudo apt-get update
```

```
sudo apt-get upgrade
```

```
raspi-config
```

Enable camera support in raspi-config & reboot.

Check the camera's working with these two test commands:

```
raspistill -o image.jpg
```

```
raspivid -o video.h264 -t 10000
```

Install software needed to send emails and attachments. (Setup a spare account @ gmail.com and enable "less secure app" access @ https://www.google.com/settings/u/0/security/lesssecureapps)

```
sudo apt-get install ssmtp
sudo apt-get install mailutils
sudo apt-get install mpack
```

Setup default settings SSMTP.

```
sudo nano /etc/ssmtp/ssmtp.conf
```

Enter this into the editor:

```
AuthUser=your-pi-gmail-account@gmail.com
AuthPass=your-user-password
FromLineOverride=YES
mailhub=smtp.gmail.com:587
UseSTARTTLS=YES
```

save file & exit.

Send a test text email and then an attachment.

```
echo "testing 1 2 3" | mail -s "Subject" you@yourdomain.co.uk
```

```
mpack -s "alarm photo" /home/pi/image.jpg you@yourdomain.co.uk
```

The standard photo resolution was too big to view on our mobile phone screen, so in the script below we've reduced the size to something easier to view on a small screen. The video that gets recorded to your SD card is still HD.

The video files captured by the script are typically too large to send as email attachments. If you want to view them remotely, it's best to login into the Pi using Filezilla in SFTP mode.

```
nano drivealarm-rpicam.sh
```

Enter the script:

```sh
#!/bin/sh
while true;  do
      valid="457624"
      scan=`./RFSniffer`
            if [ "$scan" = "$valid" ]; then
                  d=`date +%d%m%y`
                  t=`date +%T`
                  raspistill -o $t$d.jpg -w 1024 -h 768 -q 30 -hf
                  echo "Driveway alarm $t $d" | mail -s "Driveway alarm" you@gmail.com
                  echo "Driveway alarm $t $d"
                  echo "Driveway alarm $t" >> log$d.txt
                  raspivid -o $t$d.h264 -t 10000
                  mpack -s "door open photo" $t$d.jpg you@gmail.com
            else
                  echo "bad read your code and valid dont match"
                  echo $scan
            fi
      sleep 20
done
exit 0
```

Save the file (Ctrl-O) & exit (Ctrl-X).

```
chmod u+x drivealarm-rpicam.sh
```

```
sudo ./drivealarm-rpicam.sh
```

The script takes a photo & video when the PIR is triggered & sends the photo as an attachment to the Gmail account specified in the script. It then records 10 seconds of HD quality video to the memory card. The time of the event is also recorded to a date-stamped log file.

Here's an analysis of what happens on the raspistill command line:

```
raspistill -o $t$d.jpg -w 1024 -h 768 -q 30 -hf
```

Output a still photo to a file whose name is the current time+date.jpg. Make the photo measure 1024 pixels wide (-w) by 768 pixels high (-h). Set the quality (-q) to 30, which is quite low but reduces the size of file we then send by email. Finally, horizontal flip the picture (-hf) because our test picture was the wrong way around.

Text overlay date & time on a photo.

How to overlay text on a photo from the Raspberry Pi Camera module.

You might want to overlay text on a photo to provide a time & date stamp, before emailing the photo to your phone.

Firstly, we need to install the Imagemagick library:

```
sudo apt-get install imagemagick
```

Next, we need to take a test photo & then use the `convert` command to overlay the text.

```
raspistill -o 1.jpg -w 1024 -h 768 -q 30
```

```
d=`date +%d%m%y`
```

```
t=`date +%T`
```

```
convert -pointsize 20 -fill yellow -draw 'text 850,30 "'$t' '$d'"' 1.jpg 2.jpg
```

As you can see in the example above, the top-left of the photo is co-ordinate 0,0 and the bottom-right would be 1024,768. The file 2.jpg is now time & date stamped.

If you notice the time & date aren't set correctly, you can run:

```
sudo dpkg-reconfigure tzdata
```

The script below will email you a time & date stamped photo:

```
while true;  do
      valid="457624"
      scan=`./RFSniffer`
           if [ "$scan" = "$valid" ]; then
      d=`date +%d%m%y`
      t=`date +%T`
      raspistill -o 1.jpg -w 1024 -h 768 -q 30
      raspivid -o $d$t.h264 -t 10000
      convert -pointsize 20 -fill yellow -draw 'text 850,30 "'$t' '$d'"' 1.jpg $d$t.jpg
      mpack -s "alarm photo" /home/pi/$d$t.jpg you@youremailaddress.co.uk

           else
                echo "bad read your code and valid dont match"
                echo $scan
           fi
      sleep 20
done
exit 0
```

This script is called drivealarm-rpicamtd.sh

23

How to attach a buzzer to the Raspberry Pi.

Cheap 5 volt buzzer modules are available on eBay for around £1 and connect to a GPIO pin & GND on the Raspberry Pi. If you set the GPIO pin high, the buzzer emits a noise, and when you set the GPIO pin back to 0 it stops. Make sure you wire the buzzer the right way around (shorter leg to gnd, longer leg to GPIO pin 18). The wires can be different colours.

Here's how you connect it to the Model B Raspberry Pi.

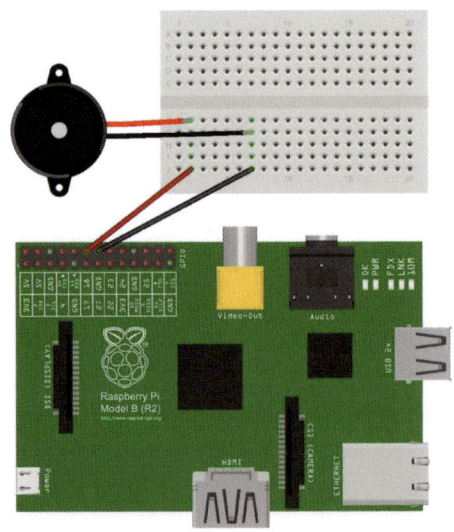

And the B+ & Pi 3

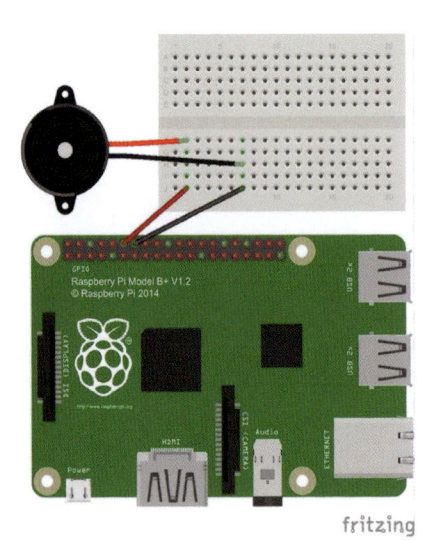

Here's a script called buzzer.sh, that will turn the buzzer on & off twice. It gets pulled down from our server with the other scripts.

24

```
#!/bin/sh

echo "18" > /sys/class/gpio/export
echo "out" > /sys/class/gpio/gpio18/direction

	echo "1" > /sys/class/gpio/gpio18/value
	sleep .5
	echo "0" > /sys/class/gpio/gpio18/value
	sleep .5
	echo "1" > /sys/class/gpio/gpio18/value
	sleep .5
	echo "0" > /sys/class/gpio/gpio18/value


echo "18" > /sys/class/gpio/unexport
```

There are also three other individual buzzer patterns, in buzzer2.sh, buzzer3.sh & buzzer4.sh. The last two scripts use a loop to achieve more complicated patterns. If you have a combination of doorbells & PIR sensors, it's good to have a different noise for each.

You can test the buzzer, by typing in:

```
sudo ./buzzer.sh
```

add the line

```
./buzzer.sh &
```

to an existing script to sound the buzzer. The & ampersand character makes the buzzer command run in the background, so it doesn't delay the rest of the script.

As you can see, the buzzer & the 433MHz receiver fit comfortably on the same mini breadboard. Remember the longer leg on the buzzer is the + side, shorter leg is GND.

How to play an MP3 file when the doorbell is pressed.

```
#!/bin/sh
while true;  do
        valid="457624"
        scan=`./RFSniffer`
                if [ "$scan" = "$valid" ]; then
                        omxplayer -o local Doorbell.mp3
                else
                        echo "bad read your code and valid dont match"
                        echo $scan
                fi
        sleep 20
done
exit 0
```

If you have a set of speakers plugged into the 3.5mm headphone output on the Pi, the script listed above will play an MP3 file when the doorbell is pressed. The line highlighted in red can be placed in any of the other scripts.

You can download example MP3 bells, gongs & sirens to experiment with:

`wget securipi.co.uk/sounds.zip`

`unzip sounds.zip`

`ls *.mp3`

To play an MP3 file to the 3.5mm headphone output

`omxplayer -o local Doorbell.mp3`

and to play an MP3 file through the HDMI port on your TV

`omxplayer -o hdmi Doorbell.mp3`

an alternative MP3 audio player is mpg123

`sudo apt-get install mpg123`

`mpg123 Doorbell.mp3`

How to connect your Pi to your WiFi router using a USB WiFi dongle.

```
ifconfig
```

should show your interface wlan0 (if not reboot the Pi & make sure USB isn't plugged into a hub).

```
sudo apt-get install wpasupplicant wireless-tools
```

```
sudo nano /etc/network/interfaces
```

add this to the end of the file using the editor & save + exit.

```
allow-hotplug wlan0
iface wlan0 inet manual
wpa-roam /etc/wpa_supplicant/wpa_supplicant.conf
iface default inet dhcp
```

Command below will show you a list of WiFi hotspots in range, locate the name of your router.

```
sudo iwlist wlan0 scan | grep ESSID
```

```
sudo nano /etc/wpa_supplicant/wpa_supplicant.conf
```

Assuming your router/phone uses WPA and not the older WEP, then change the file so it reads:

```
ctrl_interface=DIR=/var/run/wpa_supplicant GROUP=netdev
update_config=1
network={
        ssid="YourSSID"
        psk="password"
        key_mgmt=WPA-PSK
}
```

Change YourSSID and password to your own versions, then save the file & reboot your Pi. Your Pi should now connect to your WiFi router.

Your Pi should automatically connect and also get the correct time & date from the NTP server, over WiFi.

If you have an Android phone (but don't have access to landline broadband) it's also able to act like a WiFi hotspot & your Pi can get online via the WiFi in your phone.

How to make your Pi automatically run our scripts at startup.

Here's how to make our scripts auto-run in the background each time you power up the Raspberry Pi, even when you don't have a screen & keyboard attached & no user is logged in. We've assumed you've already gone through all the previous chapters and have the scripts working correctly.

```
sudo nano /etc/rc.local
```

Scroll down to the bottom of the file & **above** the last line that says `exit 0` type in these lines :

```
cd home/pi/433Utils/RPi_utils
./drivealarm-rpicamtd.sh &
```

Then save the file, exit & reboot your Pi.

```
sudo reboot
```

Now, when you press the doorbell or trigger the driveway alarm you should get a photo sent to your phone's email account & if you cut the power to the Pi & let it reboot, the script should start again automatically.

If you write any of your own scripts, & want them to execute at startup time from rc.local, then it's important to make the 1st line read

```
#!/bin/sh
```

Also, when launching a script using rc.local, it doesn't know that your script is in folder /home/pi or /home/pi/433Utils/RPi_utils, which is why we first change the folder using the `cd` command. By changing folder first & then running the file, references to other files in the script will still be found.

Night & day photo emailer script for PiNoIR camera.

```sh
#!/bin/sh

while true; do
        valid="457624"
        scan=`./RFSniffer`
        HOUR="$(date +'%H')"


        if [ "$scan" = "$valid" -a $HOUR -ge 21 -o "$scan" = "$valid" -a $HOUR -lt 07 ]; then
                echo "taking a Night-time photo"
                d=`date +%d%m%y`
                t=`date +%T`
                raspistill -ex night -o 1.jpg -w 1024 -h 768 -q 30
                raspivid -ex night -o $d$t.h264 -t 50000
                convert -pointsize 20 -fill yellow -draw 'text 850,30 "'$t' '$d'"' 1.jpg $d$t.jpg
                mpack -s "Night-time alarm photo" $d$t.jpg youremailaddress@gmail.com
                rm 1.jpg
        elif [ "$scan" = "$valid" ]; then
                echo "taking a Daytime photo"
                ./buzzer.sh
                d=`date +%d%m%y`
                t=`date +%T`
                raspistill -o 1.jpg -w 1024 -h 768 -q 30
                raspivid -o $d$t.h264 -t 10000
                convert -pointsize 20 -fill yellow -draw 'text 850,30 "'$t' '$d'"' 1.jpg $d$t.jpg
                mpack -s "Daytime alarm photo" $d$t.jpg youremailaddress@gmail.com
                rm 1.jpg
        else
                echo "BAD READ:  your code and the valid don't match"
                echo "Your correct valid code should be " $scan
        fi
        sleep 5
done
exit 0
```

The script drivealarm-night.sh is pulled down from our server with the other scripts. It's really only useful if you have the PiNoIR camera module without the infrared filter on it.

It the hour is greater than or equal to 21 or less than 07 (so between 21:00 & 6:59) it takes a photo & video using night settings, otherwise it takes the photo in regular mode. You can adjust the start & end hours in the first IF statement, to suit the time of day it gets dark & light.

The night settings on the Raspberry PiNoIR camera basically use a longer exposure time, so while you get much more light in the photo than if you'd used the regular Pi camera, you'll notice that anyone moving in darkness will appear to leave a streak, and you won't be able to make out faces unless they stand completely still for several seconds. If you've got plenty of night IR illumination then experiment with regular exposure at night, rather than night exposure.

A script that detects a doorbell & a PIR sensor.

```sh
#!/bin/sh

while true;  do
        valid="457624"
        valid2="789789"
        scan=`./RFSniffer`
        HOUR="$(date +'%H')"

        if [ "$scan" = "$valid" ]; then
                echo "Doorbell pressed, taking photo"
                d=`date +%d%m%y`
                t=`date +%T`
                raspistill -o 1.jpg -w 1024 -h 768 -q 30
                raspivid -o $d$t.h264 -t 10000
                convert -pointsize 20 -fill yellow -draw 'text 850,30 "'$t' '$d'"' 1.jpg $d$t.jpg
                mpack -s "Doorbell pressed" $d$t.jpg youremailaddress@gmail.com
                rm 1.jpg
        elif [ "$scan" = "$valid2" ]; then
                echo "PIR motion detected, taking photo"
                d=`date +%d%m%y`
                t=`date +%T`
                raspistill -o 1.jpg -w 1024 -h 768 -q 30
                raspivid -o $d$t.h264 -t 10000
                convert -pointsize 20 -fill yellow -draw 'text 850,30 "'$t' '$d'"' 1.jpg $d$t.jpg
                mpack -s "PIR motion detected" $d$t.jpg youremailaddress@gmail.com
                rm 1.jpg
        else
                echo "BAD READ:   your code and the valid don't match"
                echo "Your correct valid code should be " $scan
        fi
        sleep 5
done
exit 0
```

The script drivealarm-multi.sh is pulled down from our server with the other scripts. It's really only useful if you have more than one device you want to detect from – say a Lloytron MIP doorbell & a PIR module.

You can extend the script by copying & pasting the elif statement block (highlighted in red) & creating valid3 & valid4 variables.

Using a Sony PS2 or PS3 Eye Toy USB webcam to take photos.

Install software needed to send emails and attachments. (Setup a spare account @ gmail.com and log into it using the web browser on your PC at least once a month, to keep it active.)

```
sudo apt-get install ssmtp
sudo apt-get install mailutils
sudo apt-get install mpack
```

Setup default settings SSMTP.

```
sudo nano /etc/ssmtp/ssmtp.conf
```

Enter this into the editor:

```
AuthUser=your-gmail-account@gmail.com
AuthPass=your-user-password
FromLineOverride=YES
mailhub=smtp.gmail.com:587
UseSTARTTLS=YES
```

save file & exit.

Send a test text email and then an attachment.

```
echo "testing 1 2 3" | mail -s "Subject" you@yourdomain.co.uk

sudo apt-get install fswebcam
sudo fswebcam -d /dev/video0 -r 320x240 test1.jpg
sudo fswebcam -d /dev/video0 -r 640x480 test2.jpg
mpack -s "alarm photo" test1.jpg youremailaddress@gmail.com
```

Script to grab photo from webcam when door is opened.

```
nano drivealarm-webcam.sh
```

Then enter:

```
while true;  do
      valid="457624"
      scan=`./RFSniffer`
            if [ "$scan" = "$valid" ]; then
                  d=`date +%d%m%y`
                  t=`date +%T`
                  fswebcam -d /dev/video0 -r 640x480 $t$d.jpg
                  echo "Driveway Alarm $t $d" | mail -s "Driveway Alarm" you@gmail.com
                  echo "Driveway Alarm $t $d"
                  echo "Driveway Alarm $t" >> log$d.txt
                  mpack -s "Driveway Alarm photo" $t$d.jpg you@gmail.com

            else
                  echo "bad read your code and valid dont match"
                  echo $scan
            fi
      sleep 20

done
exit 0
```

Save & exit.

```
chmod u+x drivealarm-webcam.sh
```

```
sudo ./drivealarm-webcam.sh
```

Script to capture photos from Easycap USB video grabber.

When the PIR is triggered the script below will capture a series of photos from a Syntek 1160 chipset USB video grabber and save the results to the SD card. It then works out which are failed captures (under 20k in size) & deletes them. You need to use the very latest version of Raspbian to capture any good frames from the USB video grabber at all. On average, only half of the six captures will be good (increase the line `counter=6` to suit).

We still consider support for USB video grabbers on Raspberry Pi to be experimental only. This script emails the last successful capture.

```
while true;   do
      valid="457624"
      scan=`./RFSniffer`
            if [ "$scan" = "$valid" ]; then
                  d=`date +%d%m%y`
                  t=`date +%T`

      # start code for usb video grabber
      counter=6
      while [ $counter -gt 1 ]
      do

                  d=`date +%d%m%y`
                  t=`date +%T`
                  fswebcam -d /dev/video0 -i 0 -r 720x576 $d$t.jpg
                  sleep 1
                  counter=$(( $counter - 1 ))
                  echo $counter

            done
ls -l *.jpg | awk '{if ($5 < 20000) print $9}' | tee -a deletelog | xargs rm
rm deletelog
# end code for USB video grabber

                  echo "Drive Alarm $t $d" | mail -s "Drive Alarm" you@gmail.com
                  echo "Drive Alarm $t $d"
                  echo "Drive Alarm $t" >> log$d.txt
                  p=`ls *.jpg -Art | tail -n 1`
                  mpack -s "Drive Alarm photo" $p you@gmail.com

            else
                  echo "bad read your code and valid dont match"
                  echo $scan
            fi
      sleep 20
done
exit 0
```

Bluetooth scanning.

The Bluetooth adapter we used is just a cheap thumbsize unit with a CSR chip inside. To install the Bluetooth stack for Raspbian on the Pi, at the Terminal prompt type:

```
sudo apt-get install bluetooth bluez-utils blueman
```

insert the Bluetooth adapter & scan for devices by typing

```
hcitool scan
```

if it doesn't work, then use

```
hciconfig hci0 up
```

to bring the interface up & then scan again.

The shell script below writes out the unique OUI/MAC address of any Bluetooth devices it detects, when the doorbell is pressed, to a time & date stamped text file:

```
while true;  do
       valid="457624"
       scan=`./RFSniffer`
              if [ "$scan" = "$valid" ]; then

                     x=`hcitool scan --flush`
                     y=${x#*Scanning *...}
                     d=`date +%d%m%y`
                     t=`date +%T`

              echo $d,$t,$y | tr " " "\n"
              echo "-------------------"
              echo $d,$t$y | tr " " "," >> aa$d.txt
              y=''
       else
                     echo "bad read your code and valid dont match"
                     echo $scan
       fi
       sleep 20
done
exit 0
```

Set up Wifi Sniffing on Raspbian build.

```
sudo apt-get install iw tshark
sudo apt-get install subversion
sudo apt-get install libssl-dev
svn co http://svn.aircrack-ng.org/trunk aircrack-ng
cd aircrack-ng
```

```
make
sudo make install
```

```
sudo airmon-ng start wlan0
sudo tshark -i mon0 subtype probereq
```

or

```
sudo tshark -i mon0 subtype probereq -w /tmp/rpi-cap.pcap
```

or

```
sudo airodump-ng mon0
```

Scan for WiFi Probe Requests.

Earlier, we showed you how to scan for Bluetooth devices when the alarm is tripped. Many more modern phones have Bluetooth disabled by default now, but these newer Android smartphones often use WiFi to determine their location quickly, in combination with GPS.

The WiFi chip in a phone uses the same unique Mac style address (00:11:22:AB:CD:EF) as a Bluetooth chipset, so it's possible to record a unique phone identifier. You can see the unique Bluetooth & WiFi Mac addresses of your own phone under the 'Settings → About This Phone' menu.

When WiFi is turned on in my phone it sends probe requests every ten seconds. If I've previously associated successfully with other WiFi networks, then this information is also available, and may give you clues to who they are. This project works fine with the £10 WiPi USB wifi adapter available from cpc.co.uk

If you have the USB WiFi dongle connected you can use the `ifconfig` command to show information.
You should expect to see the adapter listed as `wlan0`. We now need to place the WiFi adapter into Monitor mode.

```
airmon-ng stop wlan0
```
followed by the command
```
airmon-ng start wlan0
```
should produce the `mon0` interface, you can do

```
airodump-ng mon0
```
and see WiFi access points near you. CTRL-C to quit.

To see full probe requests from devices with WiFi enabled do
```
tshark -i mon0 subtype probereq
```

This shows you the manufacturer of the device sending the probe, but it's also possible to just have the complete Mac address without the name resolution.

```
tshark -i mon0 subtype probereq -n -a duration:60 > cap.log
```
you can view the contents of the log file with
```
cat cap.log | more
```

We use the Tshark command in our script to grab the probe requests for 60 seconds, when the driveway alarm is triggered. The script also scans for Bluetooth devices. The script then processes the capture from Tshark to remove any duplicates and just leaves the unique Mac addresses spotted in the final text that are sent in the email to our Gmail account.
```
nano drivealarm-wifi.sh
```

```
while true;  do
        valid="457624"
        scan=`./RFSniffer`
              if [ "$scan" = "$valid" ]; then

                  x=`hcitool scan --flush`
                  y=${x#*Scanning *...}
                  tshark -i mon0 subtype probereq -n -a duration:60 > cap.log
                  egrep -o "[a-z0-9]{2}:[a-z0-9]{2}:[a-z0-9]{2}:[a-z0-9]{2}:[a-z0-9]{2}:[a-z0-9]{2}" cap.log > cap2.txt
                  sed '/ff:ff:ff:ff:ff:ff/d' cap2.txt > cap3.txt
                  sort -u -o cap4.txt cap3.txt
                  z=`cat cap4.txt`
                  d=`date +%d%m%y`
                  t=`date +%T`


             echo $d,$t,$y,$z | tr " " "\n"
             echo "-------------------"
             echo $d,$t,$y,$z | tr " " "," >> aa$d.txt
             echo -e "Subject: Driveway Alert\r\n\r\n ALERT $t,$y,$z" |msmtp -from=default -t you@youremailaddress.com

                  y=''
                  z=''
                  stat='0'
        else
                  echo "bad read your code and valid dont match"
                  echo $scan
              fi
        sleep 20
done
exit 0
```

Then make the file executable with
```
chmod ugo+x drivealarm-wifi.sh
```
Run the scanner command with
```
./drivealarm-wifi.sh
```

Connect to your Pi remotely from your PC.

It's a pain leaving a keyboard, mouse & monitor connected to your Pi when running the driveway alarm, so we login remotely using the free Putty terminal emulation package. Putty is available for PC, Mac & Linux from http://www.chiark.greenend.org.uk/~sgtatham/putty/download.html
This gives you a remote text terminal window on your PC, where you can issue commands as if you were sat in front of the Pi.

When you first install Raspbian Wheezy onto an SD card & start your Pi, you'll notice the `raspi-config` command will give you the option to turn on SSH – this is the service we use to login remotely. When you boot up the Pi, you'll also see the IP Address allocated to your Pi, above the Login & Password prompt – it will look something like 192.168.1.149 ← *note down the address you see and enter it into the Putty software on your PC.*

If you don't see the ip address you can use the command:

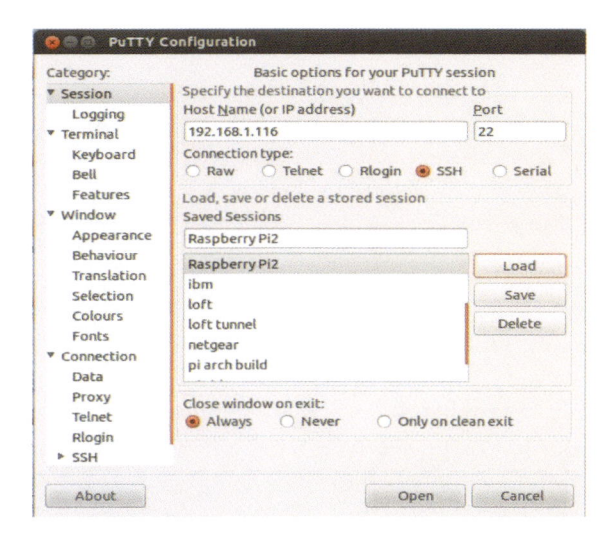

```
sudo ifconfig
```
On the PC running Putty, make sure the IP address is entered, you are set to Port 22 & the SSH radio button is selected, choose Open. Login as *pi* & password *raspberry*. Once logged in use `passwd` to change the easily guessed default to something else. We suggest you also do `sudo su` and `passwd` again, to change the root password, then do CTRL-D to drop back to user Pi.

You can make the scripts you've created run in background on the Pi & then logout from Putty. You do this by adding an ampersand character '&' to the end. To run scanner.sh in background type:

```
./scanner.sh &
```

Make a note of the process number displayed (say 2501 for example below) & then logout using CTRL-D. You should now receive emails from your Pi every time the alarm is tripped.

When you log back in you can kill the background process by rebooting the Pi, or by doing:

```
sudo kill -9 2501
```

How to transfer files from your Pi to PC using Filezilla.

On your Raspberry Pi type in

```
ifconfig
```

and make a note of your inet addr of eth0 interface, it will be something like 192.168.1.135

On your PC, Mac or Linux PC download & install Filezilla from
https://filezilla-project.org/download.php

Launch Filezilla & go to File → Site Manager → New Site → name it Raspberry Pi.

Then enter the following, remembering your IP address won't be the same as mine:
Host   : 192.168.1.135
Port   : 22
Protocol   : SFTP
Logon Type   : Normal
Login   : pi
Password   : raspberry

Then click OK.

File → Site Manager → Raspberry Pi → Connect → tick always trust this host tickbox & OK. List of files on the Pi appears in the right hand pane. You can drag videos captured on your Pi onto your PC's Desktop (left hand pane).

Once you have the H.264 video files on your PC, you can play them using the free VLC Media Player. http://www.videolan.org/vlc/index.html

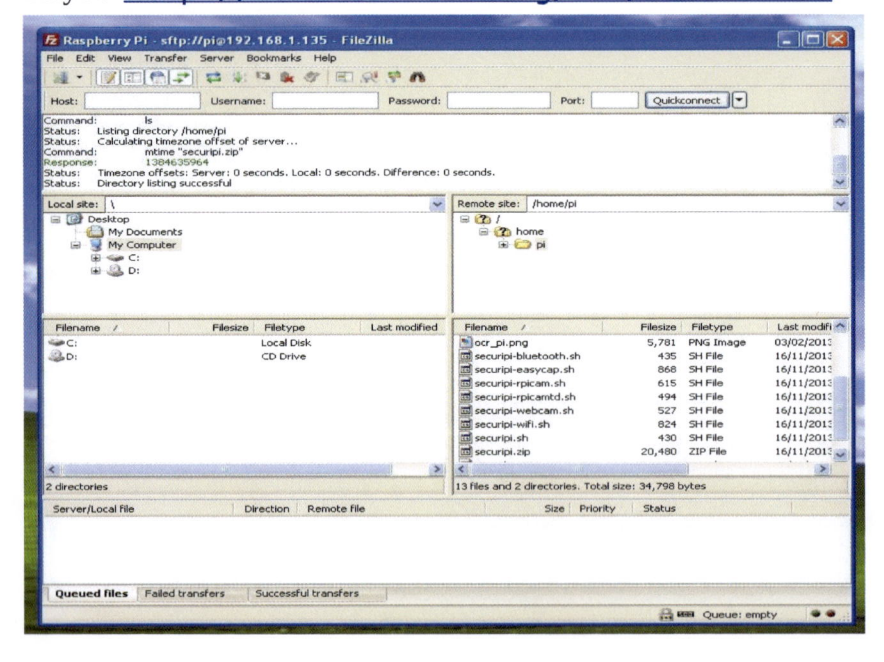

Reverse Engineering Wireless Gadgets

How to receive codes from a wireless remote on your Raspberry Pi.

This guide will show you how to receive signals from most remote control gadgets that use the 433MHz (Europe) and 315MHz (North America) bands. The software will only receive AM signals that are transmitted using Manchester / OOK type encoding scheme.

You need a suitable 433MHz or 315MHz receiver board connected to your Pi. The really cheap boards can only receive signals from up to 3 metres away. A decent crystal-controlled shielded super-heterodyne board only costs a few extra £s, and will pick up signals through walls from a 20 metre distance. http://www.ebay.co.uk/itm/161662463558

The receiver boards usually have three pins labelled 5V, GND and Data. The PiGPIO library and Python script looks for a connection on GPIO 20 by default, which is fine if you own a Pi A+, B+, Pi2, Pi3 or Pi Zero. If you have an older model B Pi, with less GPIO pins, you should edit the _433.py Python script so it looks for a connection on RX27 (GPIO27) instead of RX20 (GPIO20).

Here's how the 433Mhz receiver connects to GPIO20 on the A+, B+,Pi2, Pi 3 or Pi Zero.

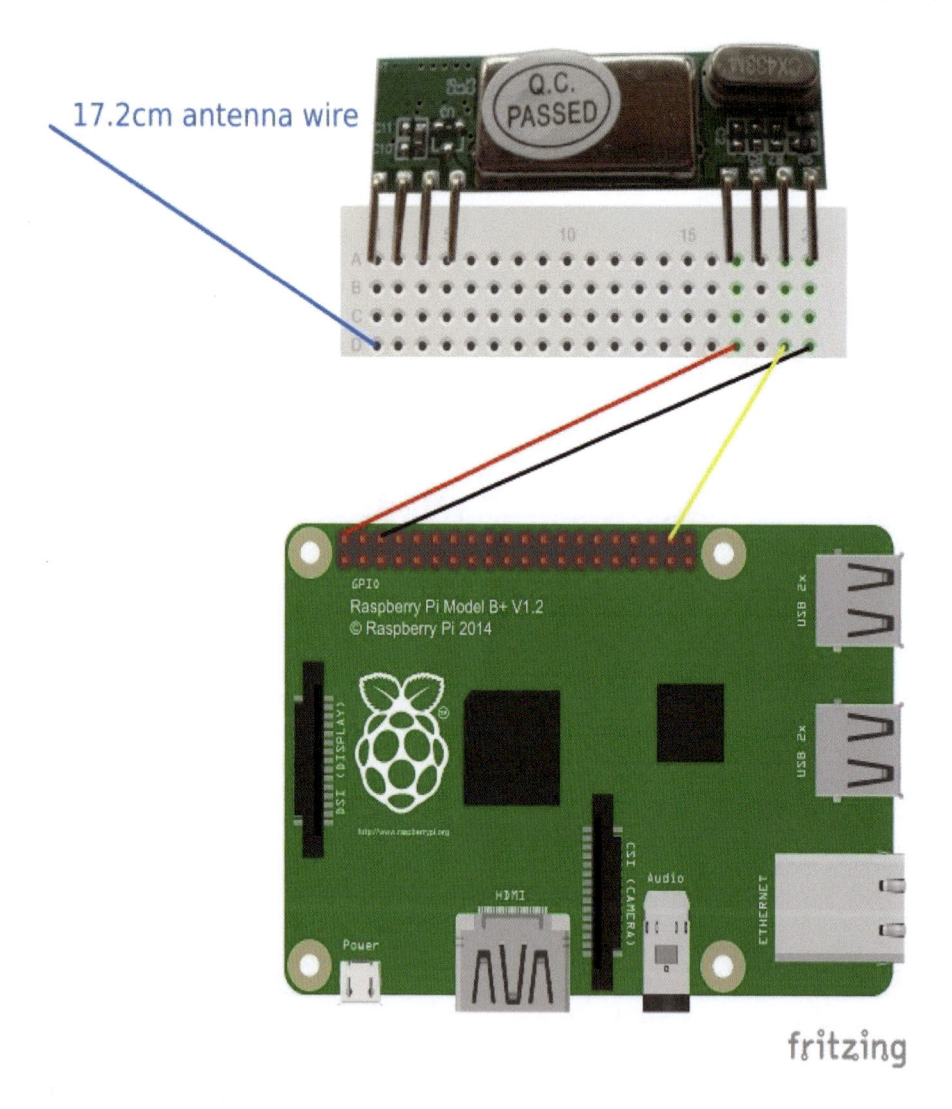

Here's how the receiver connects to a Pi model B on GPIO27

40

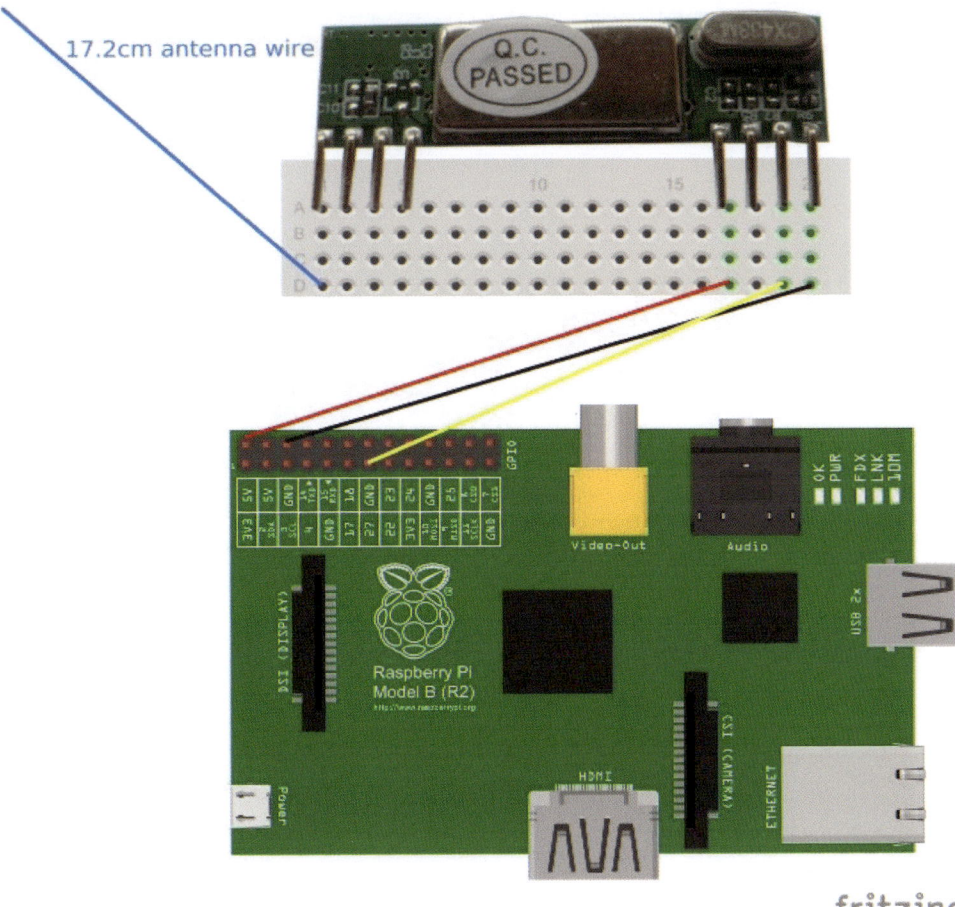

Firstly you need to install PiGPIO

```
wget abyz.me.uk/rpi/pigpio/pigpio.zip
unzip pigpio.zip
cd PIGPIO
make
sudo make install
```

It takes several minutes to "make" the software. Then launch the PiGPIO daemon with

```
sudo pigpiod
```

Next we need to grab the Python code for 433 decoding

```
wget abyz.me.uk/rpi/pigpio/code/_433_py.zip
```

```
unzip _433_py.zip
```

```
python _433.py
```

If you now press the buttons on your remote control you should see the codes produced on-screen.

```
pi@raspberrypi ~/pigpio/PIGPIO $ python _433.py
code=5592332 bits=24 (gap=10270 t0=335 t1=997)
code=5592332 bits=24 (gap=10270 t0=334 t1=998)
code=5592332 bits=24 (gap=10270 t0=335 t1=997)
code=5592332 bits=24 (gap=10269 t0=334 t1=998)
code=5592332 bits=24 (gap=10270 t0=334 t1=998)
code=5592332 bits=24 (gap=10271 t0=334 t1=998)
code=5592512 bits=24 (gap=10270 t0=335 t1=999)
code=5592512 bits=24 (gap=10275 t0=335 t1=999)
code=5592512 bits=24 (gap=10275 t0=334 t1=999)
code=5592512 bits=24 (gap=10270 t0=335 t1=998)
code=5592512 bits=24 (gap=10270 t0=334 t1=999)
code=5592512 bits=24 (gap=10270 t0=334 t1=998)
code=5592323 bits=24 (gap=10275 t0=335 t1=999)
code=5592323 bits=24 (gap=10275 t0=335 t1=999)
code=5592323 bits=24 (gap=10275 t0=335 t1=999)
code=5592323 bits=24 (gap=10275 t0=336 t1=998)
code=5592368 bits=24 (gap=10270 t0=335 t1=999)
code=5592368 bits=24 (gap=10275 t0=335 t1=999)
code=5592368 bits=24 (gap=10275 t0=335 t1=999)
code=5592368 bits=24 (gap=10275 t0=335 t1=999)
```

A variety of information is produced. The gap=, t0= and t1= values are useful if you want to re-transmit the codes you've received. The only information needed for receiving is the code= part.

The _433.py program runs for 60 seconds and then quits. Most remotes transmit the same code several times in a row, as a protection against wireless interference.

The codes that start 5592 are all produced by a simple 4 button 433MHZ remote control. I've written them down, along with the button they correspond to, and will use them in a shell script that interacts with a patched version of _433.py that I've called r433.py. I only changed a couple of lines:

```python
    for i in range(args-1):
        print("sending {}".format(sys.argv[i+1]))
        tx.send(int(sys.argv[i+1]))
        time.sleep(1)

    tx.cancel() # Cancel the transmitter.

    time.sleep(0.5)

    rx.cancel() # Cancel the receiver.

    pi.stop() # Disconnect from local Pi.
```

42

you can pull the r433.py and 433test.sh commands down from our server with

```
wget http://www.securipi.co.uk/r433.py
```

and

```
wget http://www.securipi.co.uk/433test.sh
```

make the shell script executable with

```
chmod a+x 433test.sh
```

run the script with

```
./433test.sh
```

```
#!/bin/sh
while true; do
        a="5592332"
        b="5592512"
        c="5592323"
        d="5592368"
        scan=`python r433.py | head -n 1`
#       echo $scan

        if [ "$scan" = "$a" ]; then
                echo "You pressed A"

        elif [ "$scan" = "$b" ]; then
                echo "You pressed B"

        elif [ "$scan" = "$c" ]; then
                echo "You pressed C"

        elif [ "$scan" = "$d" ]; then
                echo "You pressed D"


        fi
done
exit
```

Transmitting signals.

When we ran the _433.py receiver software we saw the code, bits, gap and t0 and t1 values for our remote control. If you wrote those down it's possible to use a 433Mhz transmitter module, to replay those codes using the Raspberry Pi.

The transmitter module has 3 pins: 5 volt, ground GND and Data. The data pin attaches to GPIO 21, below the receiver data pin 20. 5 volt and ground also attach to spare pins on the Pi.

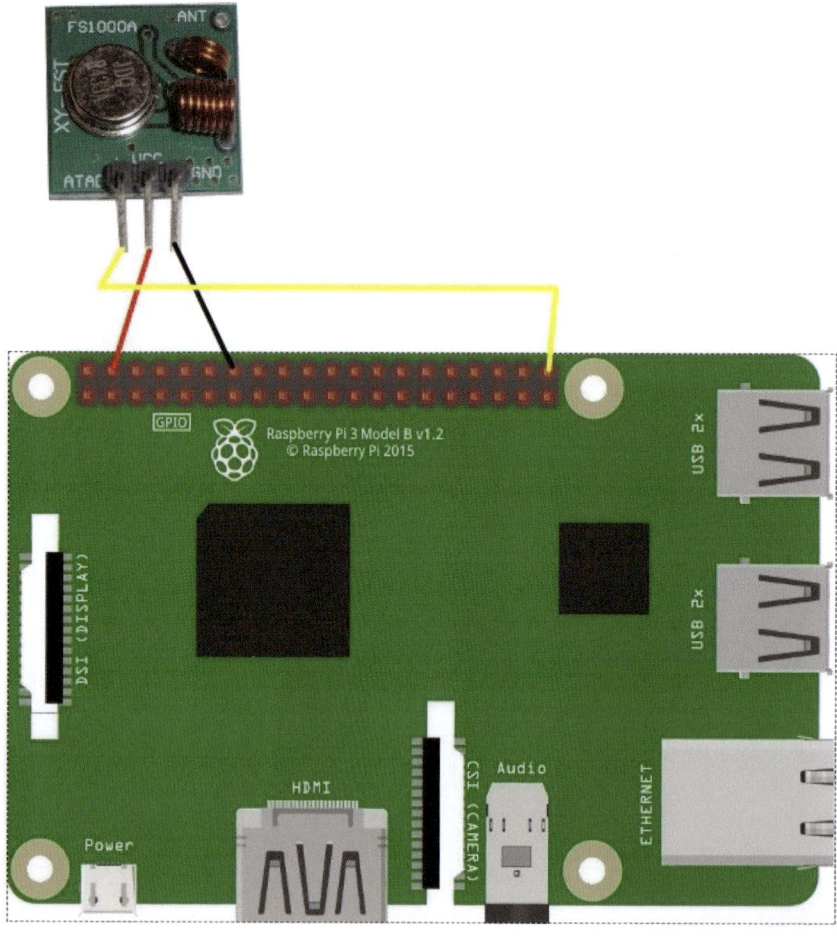

We've written a small python script that displays a menu of buttons on the desktop, and currently emulates the 4 button remote control transmitter keyfob seen here:
https://www.amazon.co.uk/dp/B01DOJ9XEW

44

Pull the code down from our server with:

```
wget http://www.securipi.co.uk/xmit.py
```

and run it on your Pi's desktop by opening a terminal window and typing

```
python xmit.py
```

You can modify the code to contain your own gadget's codes, gap, T0 and T1 settings.

```
#!/usr/bin/env python
# by Twitter user @SecuriPi
from Tkinter import *
import os
import subprocess
import sys
import time
import pigpio
import _433

RX=20
TX=21
pi = pigpio.pi()


def preset1():
    code=5592512
    tx=_433.tx(pi, gpio=TX, gap=13885, t0=444, t1=1354)
    tx.send(code)
    tx.cancel()

def preset2():
    code=5592368
    tx=_433.tx(pi, gpio=TX, gap=13885, t0=444, t1=1354)
    tx.send(code)
    tx.cancel()

def preset3():
    code=5592332
    tx=_433.tx(pi, gpio=TX, gap=13885, t0=444, t1=1354)
    tx.send(code)
    tx.cancel()

def preset4():
    code=5592323
    tx=_433.tx(pi, gpio=TX, gap=13885, t0=444, t1=1354)
    tx.send(code)
    tx.cancel()

master = Tk()
label = Label(master, text="433Mhz Transmitter", fg="red", height=3)
label.grid(row=0, column=0, columnspan=2, sticky=N+S+E+W)
Button(master, text='A', command=preset1).grid(row=2, column=0, sticky=W+E)
Button(master, text='B', command=preset2).grid(row=2, column=1, sticky=W+E)
Button(master, text='C', command=preset3).grid(row=3, column=0, sticky=W+E)
Button(master, text='D', command=preset4).grid(row=3, column=1, sticky=W+E)

mainloop()
```

This is the python script xmit.py running on the Pi's desktop. You can use it to send button codes to the receiver module that came with the 433Mhz keyfob.

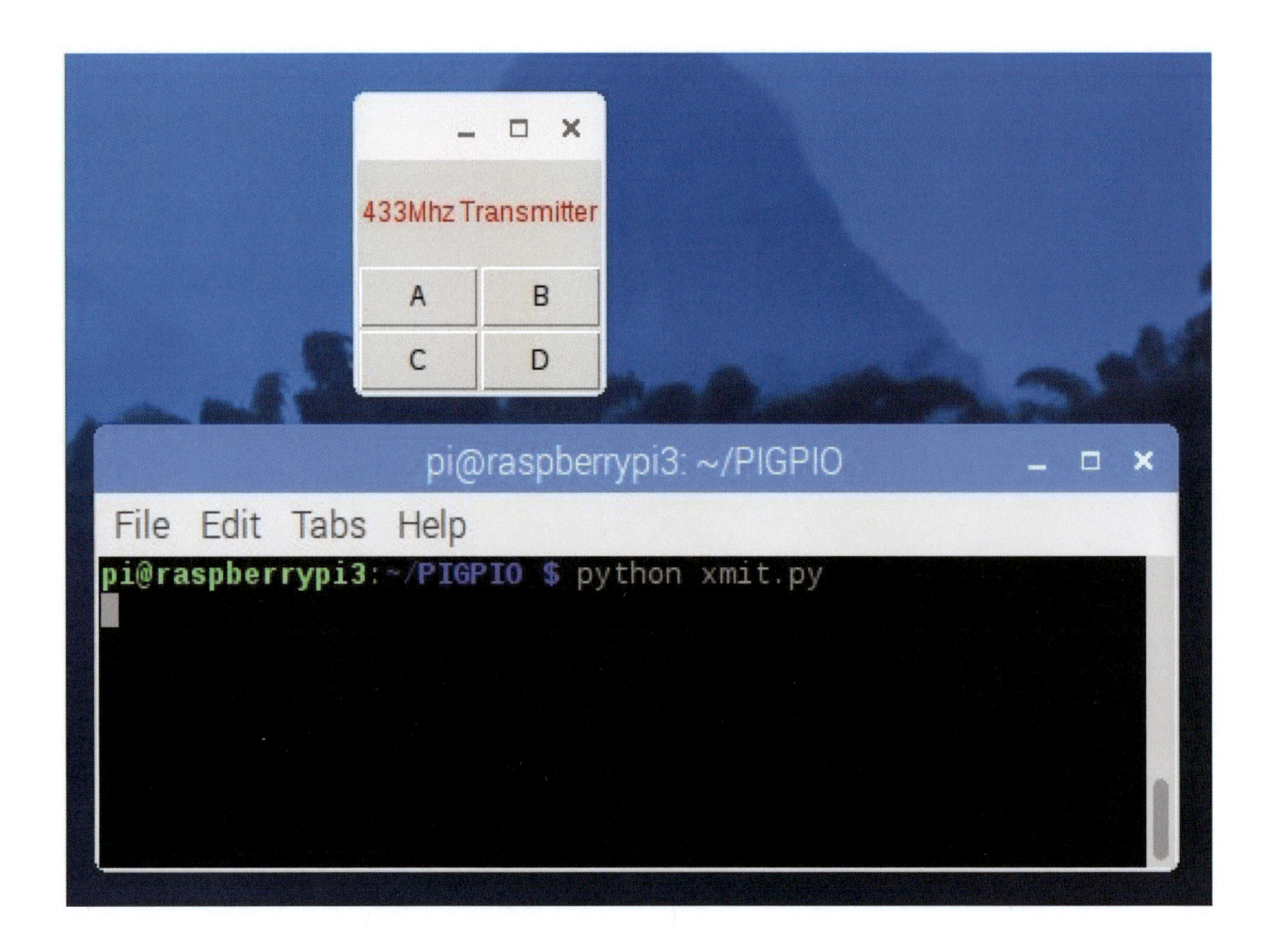

46

Remote control mains sockets.

In this chapter we'll look at using the Raspberry Pi to automatically control a 3 pack of remote control mains sockets, that we've bought from eBay.

We've made a new receiver script called testrx1.py which prints out detected codes from 433.92Mhz wireless gadgets and also stores them in a comma-delimited file called 433log.txt.

```
import sys
import time
import pigpio
import _433
from time import sleep
from signal import pause

RX=20
pi = pigpio.pi()
def rx_callback(code, bits, gap, t0, t1):
   print("code={} bits={} (gap={} t0={} t1={})".
      format(code, bits, gap, t0, t1))
   file = open("433log.txt","a")
   file.write(str(code)+',')
   file.write(str(bits)+',')
   file.write(str(gap)+',')
   file.write(str(t0)+',')
   file.write(str(t1)+'\n')
   file.close()

_433.rx(pi, gpio=RX, callback=rx_callback)
```

```
pause()
```

Assuming you've got already got the PIGPIO daemon running (sudo pigpiod), run the python receiver script with:

```
python testrx1.py
```

When we press the on and off buttons for sockets 1 and 2 we get this output.

```
pi@raspberrypi3:~/PIGPIO $ python testrx1.py
code=9775839 bits=24 (gap=9580 t0=300 t1=884)
code=9775839 bits=24 (gap=9585 t0=306 t1=879)
code=9775839 bits=24 (gap=9615 t0=304 t1=880)
code=9775839 bits=24 (gap=9590 t0=304 t1=881)
code=9775838 bits=24 (gap=9580 t0=300 t1=884)
code=9775838 bits=24 (gap=9585 t0=300 t1=885)
code=9775838 bits=24 (gap=9605 t0=307 t1=878)
code=9775838 bits=24 (gap=9625 t0=301 t1=883)
code=9775838 bits=24 (gap=9595 t0=300 t1=884)
code=9775837 bits=24 (gap=9585 t0=300 t1=884)
code=9775837 bits=24 (gap=9585 t0=302 t1=883)
code=9775837 bits=24 (gap=9610 t0=300 t1=884)
code=9775837 bits=24 (gap=9585 t0=300 t1=884)
code=9775836 bits=24 (gap=9580 t0=300 t1=884)
code=9775836 bits=24 (gap=9581 t0=299 t1=885)
code=9775836 bits=24 (gap=9590 t0=302 t1=883)
code=9775836 bits=24 (gap=9625 t0=299 t1=885)
code=9775836 bits=24 (gap=9600 t0=299 t1=885)
```

You can inspect the 433log.txt file with

```
cat 433log.txt
```

or

```
nano 433log.txt
```

```
pi@raspberrypi3:~/PIGPIO $ cat 433log.txt
9775839,24,9580,300,884
9775839,24,9585,306,879
9775839,24,9615,304,880
9775839,24,9590,304,881
9775838,24,9580,300,884
9775838,24,9585,300,885
9775838,24,9605,307,878
9775838,24,9625,301,883
9775838,24,9595,300,884
9775837,24,9585,300,884
9775837,24,9585,302,883
9775837,24,9610,300,884
9775837,24,9585,300,884
9775836,24,9580,300,884
9775836,24,9581,299,885
9775836,24,9590,302,883
9775836,24,9625,299,885
9775836,24,9600,299,885
pi@raspberrypi3:~/PIGPIO $
```

On the previous two screens we could see that the last two digits of the Code would change each time we pressed a button, so:

9775839 = socket 1 on
9775838 = socket 1 off
9775837 = socket 2 on
9775836 = socket 2 off

The bits were always set to 24. The Gap, T0 and T1 values changed around a little but are basically all near enough that you could choose any set and they'll work with all the Code values.

This next script allows us to turn the sockets on and off at preset times using a Python script on the Raspberry Pi.

```
nano timer.py
```

```python
import sys
import time
import pigpio
import _433
import datetime
import os
import subprocess

TX=21
pi = pigpio.pi()

def on1():
    code=9775839
    tx=_433.tx(pi, gpio=TX, gap=9580, t0=299, t1=885)
    tx.send(code)
    tx.cancel()

def off1():
    code=9775838
    tx=_433.tx(pi, gpio=TX, gap=9580, t0=299, t1=885)
    tx.send(code)
    tx.cancel()

def on2():
    code=9775837
    tx=_433.tx(pi, gpio=TX, gap=9580, t0=299, t1=885)
    tx.send(code)
    tx.cancel()

def off2():
    code=9775836
    tx=_433.tx(pi, gpio=TX, gap=9580, t0=299, t1=885)
    tx.send(code)
    tx.cancel()
```

```
while True:
    now = datetime.datetime.now()
    if now.hour == 19 and now.minute == 47 and now.second == 00:
        print 'Turning socket 1 on'
        on1()
        time.sleep(2)
    elif now.hour == 19 and now.minute == 49 and now.second == 00:
        print 'Turning socket 1 off'
        off1()
        time.sleep(2)
    if now.hour == 19 and now.minute == 54 and now.second == 00:
        print 'Turning socket 2 on'
        on2()
        time.sleep(2)
    elif now.hour == 19 and now.minute == 54 and now.second == 20:
        print 'Turning socket 2 off'
        off2()
        time.sleep(2)
```

run it with :

```
python timer.py
```

The script turns socket 1 on at 19:47:00 and off again two minutes later. It also turns socket 2 on at 19:54:00 and off again 20 seconds later.

We also made a graphical desktop widget that can control the mains adapters, called xmitmains.py, which looks like this:

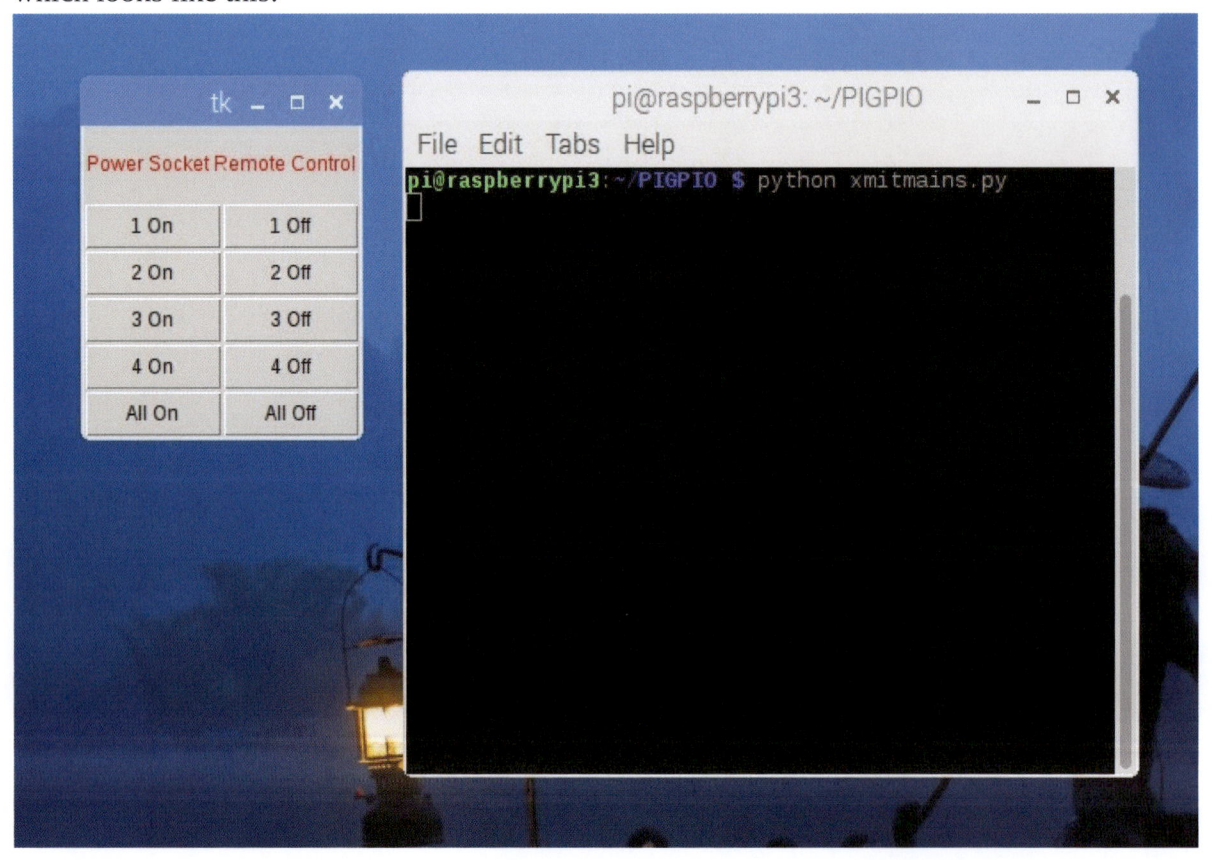

```python
#!/usr/bin/env python
# by Twitter user @SecuriPi
from Tkinter import *
import os
import subprocess
import sys
import time
import pigpio
import _433

RX=20
TX=21
pi = pigpio.pi()


def on1():
    code=9775839
    tx=_433.tx(pi, gpio=TX, gap=9580, t0=299, t1=885)
    tx.send(code)
    tx.cancel()

def off1():
    code=9775838
    tx=_433.tx(pi, gpio=TX, gap=9580, t0=299, t1=885)
    tx.send(code)
    tx.cancel()

def on2():
    code=9775837
    tx=_433.tx(pi, gpio=TX, gap=9580, t0=299, t1=885)
    tx.send(code)
    tx.cancel()

def off2():
    code=9775836
    tx=_433.tx(pi, gpio=TX, gap=9580, t0=299, t1=885)
    tx.send(code)
    tx.cancel()

def on3():
    code=9775835
    tx=_433.tx(pi, gpio=TX, gap=9580, t0=299, t1=885)
    tx.send(code)
    tx.cancel()

def off3():
    code=9775834
    tx=_433.tx(pi, gpio=TX, gap=9580, t0=299, t1=885)
    tx.send(code)
    tx.cancel()

def on4():
    code=9775831
    tx=_433.tx(pi, gpio=TX, gap=9580, t0=299, t1=885)
    tx.send(code)
    tx.cancel()
```

```python
def off4():
    code=9775830
    tx=_433.tx(pi, gpio=TX, gap=9580, t0=299, t1=885)
    tx.send(code)
    tx.cancel()

def allon():
    code=9775826
    tx=_433.tx(pi, gpio=TX, gap=9580, t0=299, t1=885)
    tx.send(code)
    tx.cancel()

def alloff():
    code=9775825
    tx=_433.tx(pi, gpio=TX, gap=9580, t0=299, t1=885)
    tx.send(code)
    tx.cancel()

master = Tk()
label = Label(master, text="Power Socket Remote Control", fg="red", height=3)
label.grid(row=0, column=0, columnspan=2, sticky=N+S+E+W)
Button(master, text='1 On', command=on1).grid(row=2, column=0, sticky=W+E)
Button(master, text='1 Off', command=off1).grid(row=2, column=1, sticky=W+E)
Button(master, text='2 On', command=on2).grid(row=3, column=0, sticky=W+E)
Button(master, text='2 Off', command=off2).grid(row=3, column=1, sticky=W+E)
Button(master, text='3 On', command=on3).grid(row=4, column=0, sticky=W+E)
Button(master, text='3 Off', command=off3).grid(row=4, column=1, sticky=W+E)
Button(master, text='4 On', command=on4).grid(row=5, column=0, sticky=W+E)
Button(master, text='4 Off', command=off4).grid(row=5, column=1, sticky=W+E)
Button(master, text='All On', command=allon).grid(row=6, column=0, sticky=W+E)
Button(master, text='All Off', command=alloff).grid(row=6, column=1, sticky=W+E)


mainloop()
```

Replaying a captured code

It's possible to have the Pi listen out for wireless codes and then offer to replay the code, without having to type in all the parameters separately. I've also added the option of replaying a different code, but with the same Gap, T0 and T1 values. There's also an option to transmit codes in a range, with a step value – so I can turn my mains sockets all off or on, 1 at a time. The script is called replay2.py

```python
#!/usr/bin/env python
import sys
import time
import pigpio
import _433
from time import sleep
from signal import pause

TX=21
RX=20
pi = pigpio.pi()

def rx_callback(code, bits, gap, t0, t1):
    if bits == 24:
        print("code={} bits={} (gap={} t0={} t1={})".
            format(code, bits, gap, t0, t1))
        # Write info to 433log.txt file
        file = open("433log.txt","a")
        file.write(str(code)+',')
        file.write(str(bits)+',')
        file.write(str(gap)+',')
        file.write(str(t0)+',')
        file.write(str(t1)+'\n')
        file.close()
        option = raw_input('replay received code y/n OR c to change the code OR input r for Range: ')
        if option == 'y':
            tx=_433.tx(pi, gpio=TX, gap=gap, t0=t0, t1=t1)
            tx.send(code)
            tx.cancel()
            pi.stop
        if option == 'c':
            code = input('enter new code to send: ')
            tx=_433.tx(pi, gpio=TX, gap=gap, t0=t0, t1=t1)
            tx.send(code)
            tx.cancel()
        if option == 'r':
            code = input('enter lowest code: ')
            endCode = input('enter highest code: ')
            stepCode = input('enter step value: ')
            while code <= endCode:
                tx=_433.tx(pi, gpio=TX, gap=gap, t0=t0, t1=t1)
                tx.send(code)
                tx.cancel()
```

```
            print('sending code '+(str(code)))
            code += stepCode
            time.sleep(1)
    else:
        print "exiting back to receiver mode"

_433.rx(pi, gpio=RX, callback=rx_callback)
pause()
```

You have to be careful when replaying codes to keep the receiver and transmitter modules more than 6 inches apart, otherwise the Gap, T0 and T1 values will inexplicably grow each time you replay the codes. (You can always look in the 433log.txt file for the original values of Gap, T0 and T1).

```
pi@raspberrypi3:~/PIGPIO $ python replay2.py
code=9775839 bits=24 (gap=9580 t0=299 t1=885)
replay received code y/n OR c to change the code OR input r for Range: c
enter new code to send: 9775838
exiting back to receiver mode
code=9775839 bits=24 (gap=9615 t0=303 t1=881)
replay received code y/n OR c to change the code OR input r for Range:
exiting back to receiver mode
code=9775839 bits=24 (gap=9595 t0=301 t1=883)
replay received code y/n OR c to change the code OR input r for Range:
exiting back to receiver mode

code=9775838 bits=24 (gap=9580 t0=301 t1=883)
replay received code y/n OR c to change the code OR input r for Range: e
code=9775838 bits=24 (gap=9595 t0=300 t1=883)
replay received code y/n OR c to change the code OR input r for Range:
exiting back to receiver mode
code=9775838 bits=24 (gap=9630 t0=302 t1=881)
replay received code y/n OR c to change the code OR input r for Range:
exiting back to receiver mode
```

The following equipment is tested & works fine with our scripts:
Lloytron MIP range of wireless Doorbell pushes, PIR movement and Magnetic Door Sensors.
Status 3 pack mains remote controlled sockets
433Mhz version of 4 button pocket keyfob transmitter/receiver for Pi and Arduino projects.

All the scripts in this PDF also work with the 315MHz equivalents used in North America.

Remote control mains relays.

If you can't use the remote control mains adapters from the previous pages to control your equipment, what are the alternatives?

You can use a wireless relay to control almost anything else. You could use one to switch the power on and off for a 5 volt Raspberry Pi, or a 12 volt LED security light, but you can also use them to switch 115v or 240v AC mains lights/appliances on and off.

If you search on eBay for "Wireless 433MHz relay" (Europe) or "Wireless 315MHz relay" (North America) you'll see lots of options. Some come with several relays on one board, some have enclosures, some come with or without remote controls.

The one pictured below cost £3/$3.50 with a 2 button remote control from a Chinese vendor on eBay. The brown 2 button remote control it came with looked just like the 4 button remote from earlier in the book, so I was hopeful that it would work fine with the scripts we've already written, even before it arrived. (You can control this relay with the 4 button xmit.py script from earlier)

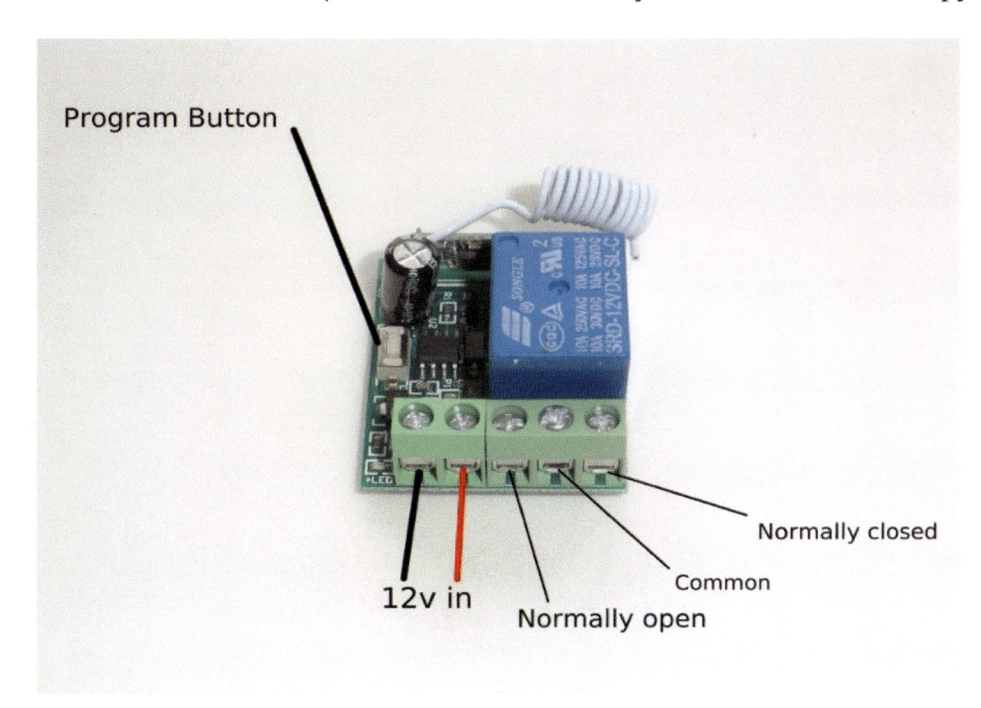

The relay board gets its power from a 12 volt source, which can be a battery or mains adapter. If you're controlling a 12 volt device, like an LED CCTV security light, you can use one power source for the relay board and the load. Otherwise you power the board from 12 volts, and keep the load separate.

The relay has several modes of operation: you can make it come on only while it senses the wireless control code and then switch off again – that's momentary mode, which you might use if operating an electronic door lock. You can also operate the relay in latch mode – where the relay receives a wireless code & switches on, then stays on until it hears the same code again.

To program momentary mode: press the program button once, and then press a button on your remote control, or transmit a code from the Raspberry Pi. To program latch mode, press the program button twice in quick succession, and press a remote control button or send a code from the Pi.

How to connect the relay to an LED panel and 12 volt battery pack.

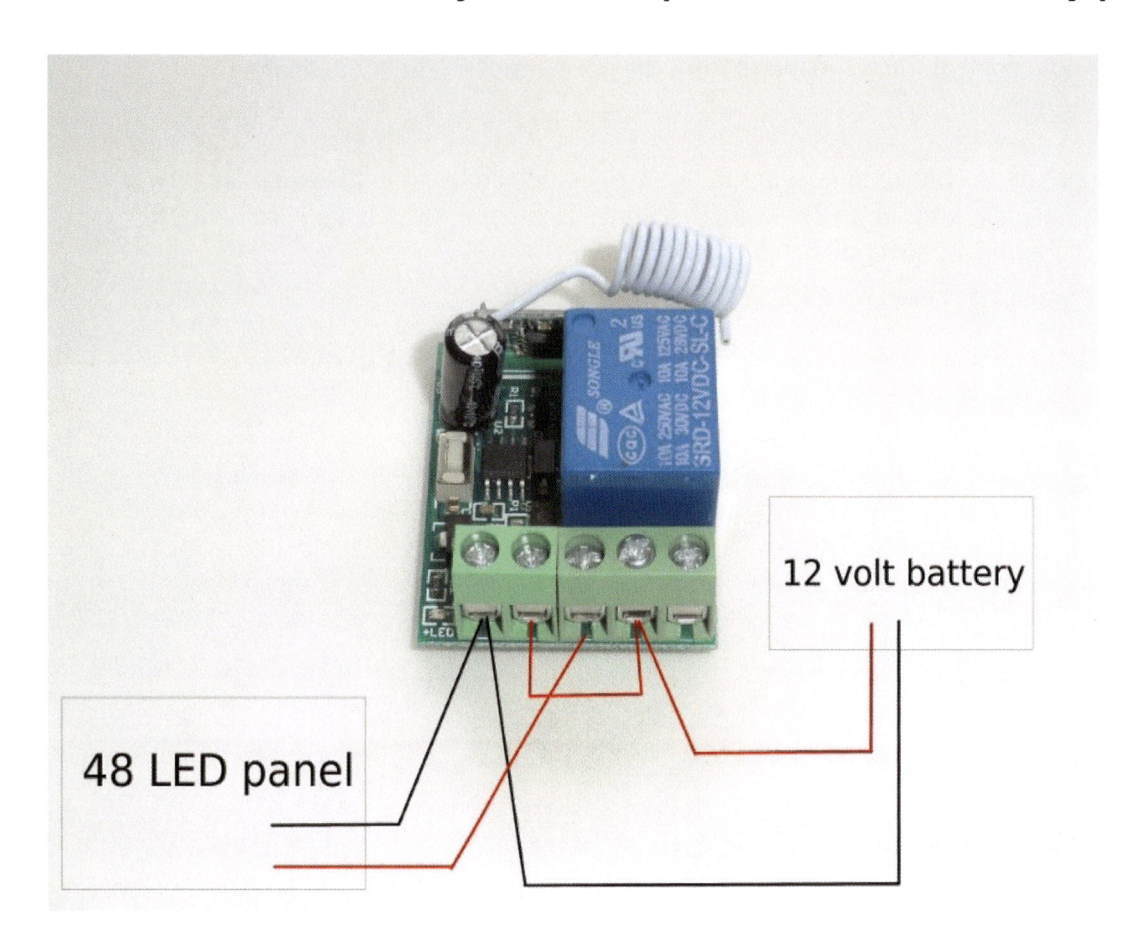

12 volt battery

48 LED panel

You can then turn the LED panel off & on with the remote control or your Raspberry Pi.

How to connect the relay to other voltages

You can connect the relay to devices that don't use 12 volts like this

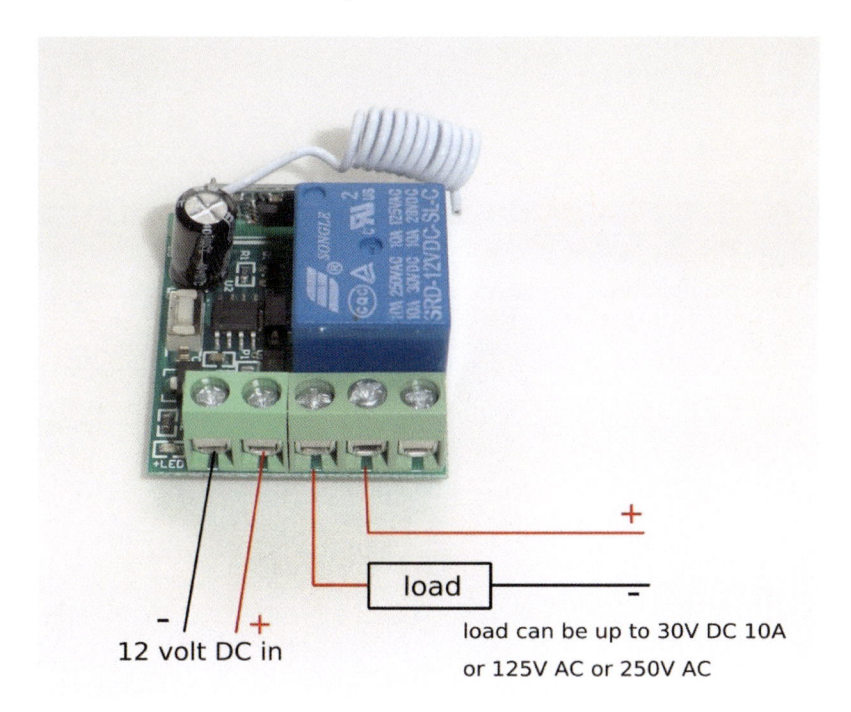

12 volt DC in

load can be up to 30V DC 10A
or 125V AC or 250V AC

If you connect a load of more than 12 volts, be aware that if you touch the underside of the board you could electrocute yourself – so be very careful and always turn the mains circuit off at the fusebox, and test the wires with a voltage multimeter, before touching anything.

DANGER! Mains voltages can kill you.

To keep things safe you can download a 3D printable enclosure for this particular relay board at http://www.thingiverse.com/thing:2246360 or wrap everything in black insulation tape.

Notes.

Make sure you remember to run the PIGPIO daemon each time you start the Pi (sudo pigpiod), or add it to your /etc/rc.local file, so it launches each time you power up the Pi.

You can buy the really good 433MHz receiver board from our eBay shop here:
http://www.ebay.co.uk/itm/161662463558

We also sell a 433Mhz transmitter/receiver pair here:
http://www.ebay.co.uk/itm/161594608707
(the transmitter is great, the receiver isn't anywhere near as good as the shielded low-noise version)

You can buy the 4 button keyfob 433Mhz version here:
http://www.ebay.co.uk/itm/131767939665

If you look in our eBay shop we also sell the 315MHz versions of each for North America.

The PiGPIO and _433.py combination works better than the usual combination of WiringPi and 433Utils, because it doesn't have fixed timings for each pulse, it works out whether it's seeing a valid signal more dynamically.

Manchester encoding info : https://en.wikipedia.org/wiki/Manchester_encoding

How to control hardware from a web browser interface

Connect an LED to GPIO pin 4 and control it from a web browser

Here's how to wire an LED to the Raspberry Pi GPIO pin 4.

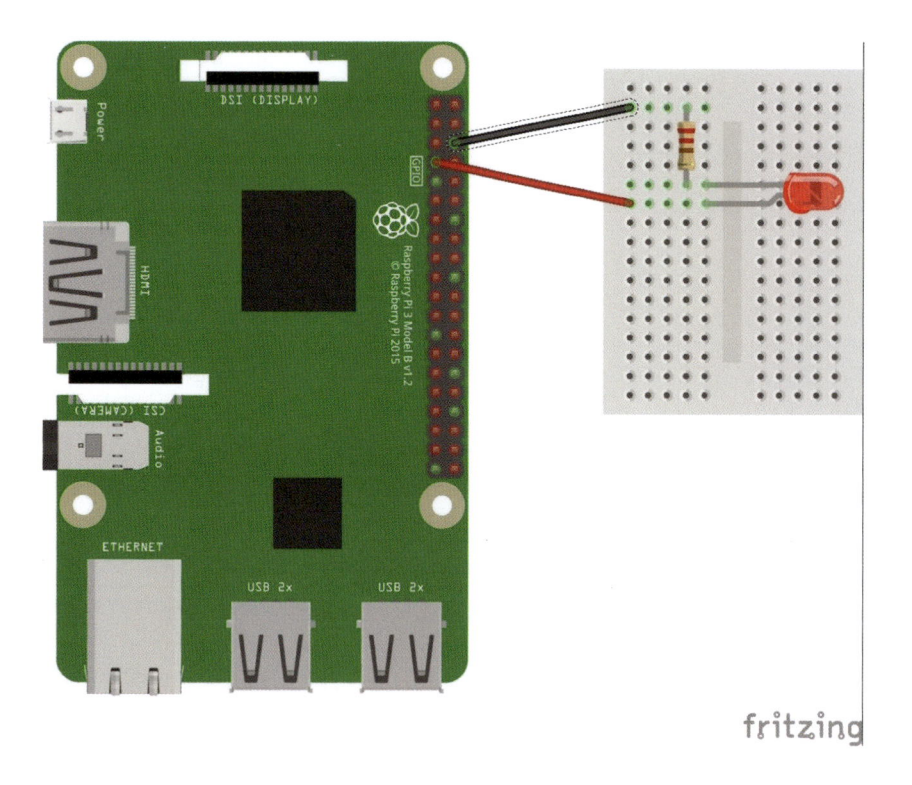

The resistor can be any value between 200 ohm and 470 ohm. The long leg of the LED connects to the GPIO4 pin (+). The short leg and flat side of the LED connect to GND (-).

Install WiringPi library

Before we go any further we need to install WiringPi, a set of utilities that make talking to the GPIO pins easier. Enter these commands at the $ terminal prompt:

```
sudo apt-get update
sudo apt-get upgrade
sudo apt-get install git-core
git clone git://git.drogon.net/wiringPi

cd wiringPi
git pull origin

./build
gpio -v
gpio readall
cd ..
```

You'll now see a list of all the GPIO assignments for Wiring Pi.

Test the LED connected to GPIO pin 4 (7 in wiringPi speak) with:

```
gpio mode 7 out
gpio write 7 1
gpio write 7 0
```

Install Apache Web Server

```
sudo apt-get update
sudo apt-get upgrade
```

```
sudo apt-get install apache2 php5 libapache2-mod-php5
```

Point a web browser at the IP address of your Pi and you should see the Apache splash screen

Setup CGI tools

```
sudo a2enmod mpm_prefork cgi
```

Restart the Apache server.

```
sudo service apache2 restart
```

We use a combination of HTML web page with Javascript image buttons on it to call the executable BASH shell scripts in CGI-BIN folder which turn the LED on GPIO pin4 on and off using WiringPi. You can edit the CGI files to perform any shell command you like.

The web page index.html file and jpg images are stored in folder

```
cd /var/www/html
```

and the cgi files are stored in folder

```
cd /usr/lib/cgi-bin
```

delete the existing Apache splash screen index.html file with

```
sudo rm /var/www/html/index.html
```

now make a new index.html file with

```
sudo nano /var/www/html/index.html
```

```html
<html>
<head>
<script Language="Javascript">
function set0()
{
    document.location="cgi-bin/set0.cgi";
}
function set1()
{
    document.location="cgi-bin/set1.cgi";
}
```

```html
</script>
</head>
<body>
    <div style="text-align:center">
    <h1>LED Toggle</h1>

<br>
    <img src="/red.jpg" id="l" onmousedown="set0()">
    <img src="/green.jpg" id="r" onmousedown="set1()">
<br>
    </div>

</body>
</html>
```

make sure the red and green jpg images files go in the same folder as index.html

```
cd   /var/www/html
sudo wget securipi.co.uk/red.jpg
sudo wget securipi.co.uk/green.jpg
cd ~
```

then find the IP address of your Raspberry Pi with

```
ifconfig
```

So in my case I'm using wired ethernet connection (eth0) and my IP address is 192.168.1.30. If I was using WiFi it would say wlan0 instead on eth0, but my IP address would be displayed in the same location. Type the IP address 192.168.1.30 into any web browser address bar on the same network and this web page should appear. (remember your IP address probably isn't 192.168.1.30)

The buttons don't do anything yet, but they will once we setup the CGI scripts.

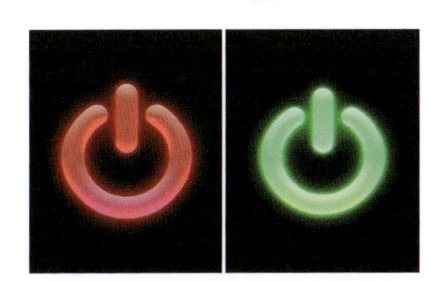

63

Setup the CGI scripts to make the web page buttons active

```
sudo nano /usr/lib/cgi-bin/set0.cgi
```

and enter

```
#!/bin/bash

gpio mode 7 out
gpio write 7 0

echo "Status: 204 No Content"
echo "Content-type: text/plain"
echo ""
```

save & quit, then

```
sudo nano /usr/lib/cgi-bin/set1.cgi
```

```
#!/bin/bash

gpio mode 7 out
gpio write 7 1

echo "Status: 204 No Content"
echo "Content-type: text/plain"
echo ""
```

Make both scripts executable with

```
sudo chmod a+x /usr/lib/cgi-bin/*.cgi
```

Now go back and refresh your web browser, and the buttons should now turn the LED on and off. If you have an Android phone connected to WiFi, bring up the Chrome web browser and type the same IP address in there and you should be able to turn the LED on and off from there too.

To make the LED controllable from anywhere with an internet connection requires a bit more work. You need to know what your external IP address is, which you can find at www.whatismyip.com

Then you need to log in to your router's setup screen, find Port Forwarding, and forward any requests for a particular outside port on your router (say 8080) to the IP address for your Pi on port 80 inside the network.

You shouldn't use port 80 for outside and inside, as port 80 externally will be scanned regularly by nefarious bots looking for exploitable servers. By using the non-standard external port of 8080 (or any number between 1024 & 32768), you are attracting less attention to your server.
Ideally you'd password protect the web page in some way, but at a minimum make sure you changed the default passwords on your Raspberry Pi for root and pi users to something other than raspberry and regularly run `sudo apt-get update` *and* `sudo apt-get upgrade`

Setup port forwarding on your router

On my router the Port Forwarding setup screen looks like this:

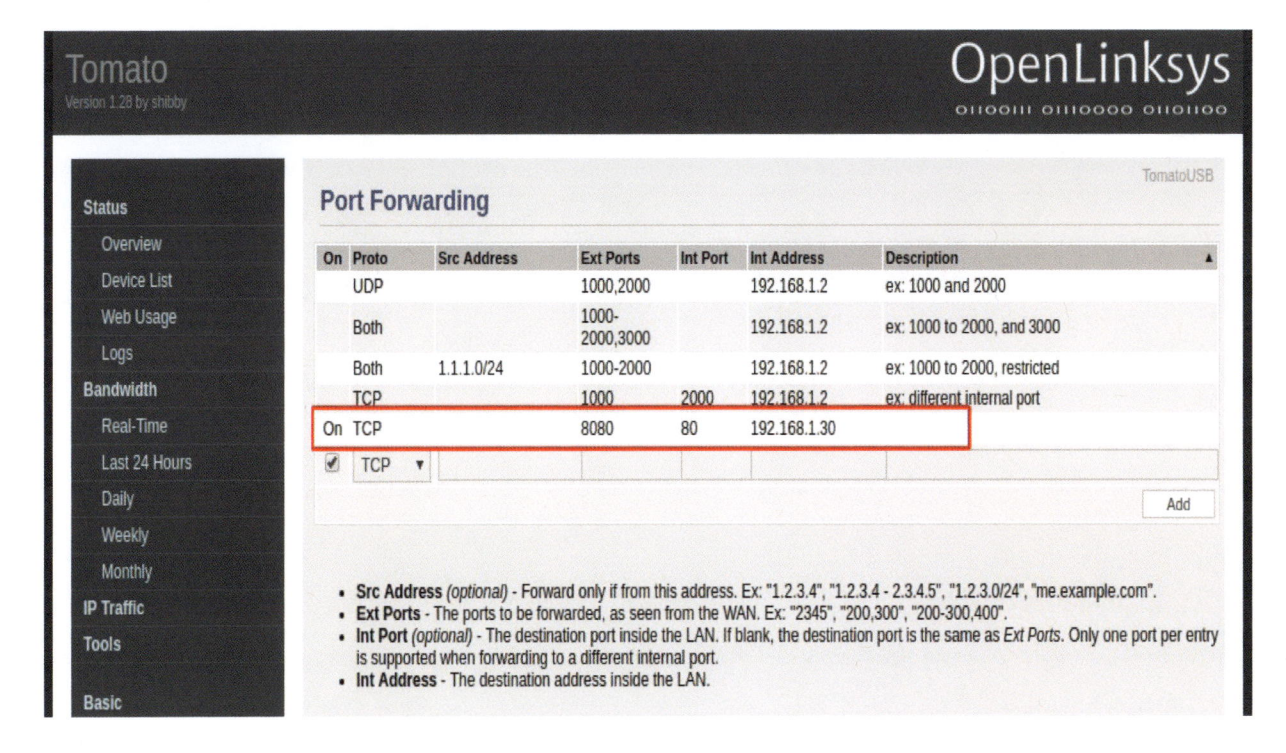

So I've opened up port 8080 externally and forward it to internal port 80 at my Raspberry Pi's static IP address of 192.168.1.30

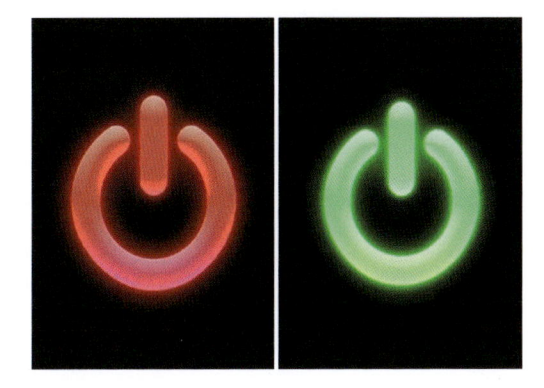

Then I opened up TOR Browser - which always uses a different IP address from your real one - and typed in my router's external IP address, a colon : , and the port number 8080, and up pops the web page running on my Pi. Now I can turn the LED on and off from anywhere in the world.

Controlling Wireless Mains Sockets from a web browser.

Now, we'll combine the ability to turn mains sockets on and off, with what we've just learnt about controlling the GPIO pins from a web browser. This chapter assumes you've followed previous chapters and have completed the mains sockets wireless control setup and LED control from a web browser, chapters. First, go to the Apache web server html folder with:

```
cd /var/www/html
```

You can pull the remote1.html file, along with the graphics down from our web server with
```
sudo wget www.securipi.co.uk/remote1html.zip
```

and extract the files with
```
sudo unzip remote1html.zip
```

then see a list of the files with
```
ls -al
```

you can examine the remote1.html web page like this:
```
sudo nano remote1.html
```

```html
<html>
<head>
<script Language="Javascript">
function set0()
{
    document.location="cgi-bin/tx1off.py";
}
function set1()
{
    document.location="cgi-bin/tx1on.py";
}
function set2()
{
    document.location="cgi-bin/tx2off.py";
}
function set3()
{
    document.location="cgi-bin/tx2on.py";
}
function set4()
{
    document.location="cgi-bin/tx3off.py";
}
function set5()
{
    document.location="cgi-bin/tx3on.py";
}
```

```
function set6()
{
    document.location="cgi-bin/tx4off.py";
}
function set7()
{
    document.location="cgi-bin/tx4on.py";
}
function set8()
{
    document.location="cgi-bin/txalloff.py";
}
function set9()
{
    document.location="cgi-bin/txallon.py";
}
</script>
</head>

<body>
    <div style="text-align:center">
    <h1>433Mhz Remote Control Mains Sockets</h1>

<br>
    <img src="/red_1.jpg" id="l" onmousedown="set0()">
    <img src="/red_2.jpg" id="l" onmousedown="set2()">
    <img src="/red_3.jpg" id="l" onmousedown="set4()">
    <img src="/red_4.jpg" id="l" onmousedown="set6()">
    <img src="/red_all.jpg" id="l" onmousedown="set8()">

<br>
    <img src="/green_1.jpg" id="r" onmousedown="set1()">
    <img src="/green_2.jpg" id="r" onmousedown="set3()">
    <img src="/green_3.jpg" id="r" onmousedown="set5()">
    <img src="/green_4.jpg" id="r" onmousedown="set7()">
    <img src="/green_all.jpg" id="r" onmousedown="set9()">
<br>
    </div>

</body>
</html>
```

Save the file and exit. Then you can enter 192.168.1.30/remote1.html into a web browser address bar (the ip address of your Pi will be different. Find it using ifconfig) and the control buttons web page will appear. The buttons don't "do" anything yet though.

Next we need to add a CGI control script for each button. Again to save time you can download them from our server.

```
cd /usr/lib/cgi-bin
```

```
sudo wget securipi.co.uk/remote1cgi.zip
```

```
sudo unzip remote1cgi.zip
```

```
sudo chmod a+x *.py
```

see a list of the CGI scripts with

```
ls -al
```

look at the first of the scripts with

```
sudo nano tx1off.py
```

```
#! /usr/bin/python
import sys
sys.path.append("/home/pi/PIGPIO")
import time
import pigpio
import _433

TX=21
pi = pigpio.pi()

code=9775838
tx=_433.tx(pi, gpio=TX, gap=9619, t0=301, t1=882)
tx.send(code)

tx.cancel()
pi.stop()
print
print "Content-type: text/plain"
print ""
```

The script above turns off socket1. To make it turn a socket on we just change the code=9775838 to a different code. If you look at the other files in this folder you'll see they're identical apart from the code they send.

If you now click refresh on your browser each button will now do something. If you get a 500 error, then you don't have the pigpio daemon running in the background, so launch it with:

```
sudo /home/pi/PIGPIO/pigpiod
```

and reload the web page again. The buttons should now transmit the 433MHz radio signal codes.

Using a PHP web page to control an LED

The previous examples using a HTML web page and CGI scripts work fine on Firefox, Chrome and Safari browers on both PC and Mac. They also work as expected on the Chrome browser on my Google Nexus Android phone. However, there's a bug in the webkit engine that sits underneath all browsers on Apple IOS devices, like iPod, iPad, and iPhone, that displays a white web page once you've clicked one of the buttons – you can press the back button, but it's still annoying. This is because the IOS browsers don't behave correctly when they see a "Status: 204 No Content" browser header (at the time of writing).

Trying to find a workaround led me to discover you can also use a PHP web page to run commands directly on the Pi. So if you're making your own home automation setup and want to control it from an iPad or iPhone, do it this way instead. Assuming you followed the previous examples already:

```
cd /var/www/html
```

```
sudo nano index2.php
```

```html
<html>
<br>
<head>
<style type="text/css">
    body { margin-top:100px; padding:0; border:0; text-align:center; background-color:#000000; }
    #title { font-family:arial; font-size:200%; color:#FFFFFF; }
    #button {-webkit-appearance: none; border:0; }
  </style>

<span id="title">LED On and Off PHP example</span>
<br>
</head>

<?php
if (isset($_POST['LightOFF']))
{
exec("/usr/lib/cgi-bin/ledoff.sh");
#echo exec("echo off");
}
if (isset($_POST['LightON']))
{
exec("/usr/lib/cgi-bin/ledon.sh");
#echo exec("echo on");
}
?>

<br>
<body>
```

```html
<div align="center">
<form method="post">
<button id="button" class="btn" name="LightOFF"><img src="red.jpg" border="0"></button> 
<button id="button" class="btn" name="LightON"><img src="green.jpg" border="0"></button>
</form>
</div>
</body>
</html>
```

You can pull this file and the .jpg images down from our server with

```
sudo wget securipi.co.uk/phpledhtml.zip
```

```
sudo unzip phpledhtml.zip
```

then go to

```
cd /usr/lib/cgi-bin
```

```
sudo wget securipi.co.uk/phpledcgi.zip
```

```
sudo unzip phpledcgi.zip
```

```
sudo chmod a+x *.sh
```

Then go to the Safari web browser on your iPad or iPhone and open 192.168.1.30/index2.php (your ip address will be different, use ifconfig to find it) and the LED should come on and off when you press the buttons, and the browser will just stay on the same page. If you have any problems, it might be you don't have WiringPi installed (see previous chapters). Here are the two shells scripts that the PHP web page calls:

ledon.sh

```
#!/bin/bash
gpio mode 7 out
gpio write 7 1
```

ledoff.sh

```
#!/bin/bash
gpio mode 7 out
gpio write 7 0
```

Using a PHP web page to remote control main sockets

This PHP version of the Remote Control Sockets web page works correctly on Apple iOS devices. I've laid the buttons out in a vertical strip, rather than horizontally, and also made the background black so the buttons appear to float on the page.

```
cd /var/www/html
```

```
sudo nano remote2.php
```

```html
<html>
<br>
<head>
<style type="text/css">
      body { margin-top:100px; padding:0; border:0; text-align:center; background-color:#000000; }
      #title { font-family:arial; font-size:200%; color:#FFFFFF; }
      #button {-webkit-appearance: none; border:0; }
   </style>

<span id="title">Remote Control Mains Sockets PHP example</span>
<br>
</head>

<?php
if (isset($_POST['tx1off']))
{
exec("/usr/lib/cgi-bin/tx1off.py");
}
if (isset($_POST['tx1on']))
{
exec("/usr/lib/cgi-bin/tx1on.py");
}

if (isset($_POST['tx2off']))
{
exec("/usr/lib/cgi-bin/tx2off.py");
}
if (isset($_POST['tx2on']))
{
exec("/usr/lib/cgi-bin/tx2on.py");
}

if (isset($_POST['tx3off']))
{
exec("/usr/lib/cgi-bin/tx3off.py");
}
```

```php
if (isset($_POST['tx3on']))
{
exec("/usr/lib/cgi-bin/tx3on.py");
}
if (isset($_POST['tx4off']))
{
exec("/usr/lib/cgi-bin/tx4off.py");
}

if (isset($_POST['tx4on']))
{
exec("/usr/lib/cgi-bin/tx4on.py");
}

if (isset($_POST['txalloff']))
{
exec("/usr/lib/cgi-bin/txalloff.py");
}

if (isset($_POST['txallon']))
{
exec("/usr/lib/cgi-bin/txallon.py");
}


?>
```

```html
<br>
<body>
<div align="center">
<form method="post">
<button id="button" class="btn" name="tx1off"><img src="red_1.jpg" border="0"></button> 
<button id="button" class="btn" name="tx1on"><img src="green_1.jpg" border="0"></button><br>

<button id="button" class="btn" name="tx2off"><img src="red_2.jpg" border="0"></button> 
<button id="button" class="btn" name="tx2on"><img src="green_2.jpg" border="0"></button><br>

<button id="button" class="btn" name="tx3off"><img src="red_3.jpg" border="0"></button> 
<button id="button" class="btn" name="tx3on"><img src="green_3.jpg" border="0"></button><br>

<button id="button" class="btn" name="tx4off"><img src="red_4.jpg" border="0"></button> 
<button id="button" class="btn" name="tx4on"><img
```

```
src="green_4.jpg" border="0"></button><br>

<button id="button" class="btn" name="txalloff"><img
src="red_all.jpg" border="0"></button> 
<button id="button" class="btn" name="txallon"><img
src="green_all.jpg" border="0"></button><br>
</form>
</div>
</body>
</html>
```

Then save and exit. Open up your web browser and point to 192.168.1.30/remote2.php (your Pi's IP address will be different, find it with ifconfig command)

If the buttons don't do anything, make sure you ran

```
sudo /home/pi/PIGPIO/pigpiod
```

and try again.

If you want to make pigpiod run automatically each time the Pi starts up, add it to /etc/rc.local with

```
sudo nano /etc/rc.local
```

and before the last line, which reads exit 0 add:

```
sudo /home/pi/PIGPIO/pigpiod
```

Save and Exit, and then reboot your Pi.

If you find the distance between your Pi and the sockets you're controlling causes a reception problem, add a 17.2cm long piece of wire to the hole on the top-right of the transmitter board marked ANT and you'll get a transmission range boost. It doesn't need to be soldered, twisting it on is fine.

If you only use the PHP version to control the sockets, then you can safely get rid of these lines from the end of each of the transmitter code Python files in /usr/lib/cgi-bin – tx1off.py etc.

```
print "Status: 204 No Content"
print "Content-type: text/plain"
print ""
```

as they're only required when using the HTML version. The PHP version still works just fine though if you leave them in.

How to stream CCTV audio over a network.

Audio capture hardware options.

The Raspberry Pi doesn't have a microphone input, so we need to use some kind of USB interface and a microphone.

There are essentially two types of microphones we're interested in: Mics that are meant to capture just the audio a couple feet around them (commonly used for Skype etc), and powered microphones with a pre-amp which capture all the audio in the environment (used for CCTV and surveillance).

If you want to add audio to your bird box project, then you could use a small USB microphone like this one (which typically cost just a few pounds from Chinese eBay sellers).

But this Mic is no good for picking up audio from more than 2 feet away – of course you can also use a USB extension lead of up to 6 metres to move this Mic nearer to your source.

It's also possible to buy USB adapters with a standard 3.5mm mic input, and you can then attach a better quality Mic to it, but again these are only for audio which is near the mic.

A CCTV microphone.

The CCTV mic is powered by a 12 volt DC supply. It contains a microphone and an amplifier. The 12V supply attaches to the red 2.1mm plug. The white phono socket attaches to a USB soundcard with a Line Level input.

CCTV mics are sometimes referred to as "room mics", because they pick-up every noise in a room very clearly.

Power supply for the CCTV Mic

We recommend that you use a 12 volt regulated & earthed power supply like this one from eBay for £11.99. It can also power Infra Red security lights. We tried several cheaper unregulated unearthed 12 volt supplies, but we always got an annoying buzzing background noise that disappeared once we used a decent power supply. It's also possible to power the Mic from a 9 or 12 volt battery pack.

USB Audio line-level capture device.

Because the CCTV mic is at line-level, you can't attach it to the Mic-In port on a laptop, PC or USB adapter, you have to use Line-In or a USB adapter with Line-In, like this one:

The Ezcap USB audio adapter works really well with the Raspberry Pi. If you wanted to, you could attach two of the CCTV microphones for recording proper stereo sound. Don't bother trying to use the cheap £3 USB mic & headphone adapters, as they're not line-level & don't work correctly.

The USB lead plugs into your Raspberry Pi and you use a male-2-male phono adapter to join the two white phono sockets together.

As you'll see below, it's possible to use this equipment & two Raspberry Pi boards to stream audio from one location to another over the internet using netcat.

There are some useful tips for voice activated recording here: http://mocha.freeshell.org/audio.html
You can download our CCTV Mic sample recording here: http://www.tpr2.co.uk/test8000.wav

Streaming Audio from one Raspberry Pi to another.

How to stream audio from one Pi to another Pi (or an Ubuntu Linux PC). We use the Netcat command to pipe the audio over a network connection from one Pi to the other.

This method uses no more than 30% of processor cycles on an old model B or A+ Pi and works flawlessly. Our preferred method of setting this up is to simultaneously SSH into each Pi remotely from our desktop PC.

On both the sending and receiving Raspberry Pi you need to install the Opus codec:

```
sudo apt-get install opus-tools
```

Discover and make a note of the IP address (here 192.168.1.39) of each Pi with the command :

```
ifconfig
```

```
pi@raspberrypi:~ $ ifconfig
eth0      Link encap:Ethernet  HWaddr b8:27:eb:81:0a:33
          inet addr:192.168.1.39  Bcast:192.168.1.255  Mask:255.255.255.0
          inet6 addr: fe80::7b52:55f5:7d60:3e81/64 Scope:Link
          UP BROADCAST RUNNING MULTICAST  MTU:1500  Metric:1
          RX packets:19164 errors:0 dropped:6 overruns:0 frame:0
          TX packets:3804 errors:0 dropped:0 overruns:0 carrier:0
          collisions:0 txqueuelen:1000
          RX bytes:1213749 (1.1 MiB)  TX bytes:2240409 (2.1 MiB)

lo        Link encap:Local Loopback
          inet addr:127.0.0.1  Mask:255.0.0.0
          inet6 addr: ::1/128 Scope:Host
          UP LOOPBACK RUNNING  MTU:65536  Metric:1
          RX packets:0 errors:0 dropped:0 overruns:0 frame:0
          TX packets:0 errors:0 dropped:0 overruns:0 carrier:0
          collisions:0 txqueuelen:0
          RX bytes:0 (0.0 B)  TX bytes:0 (0.0 B)

pi@raspberrypi:~ $
```

Tip: setup each Pi in your router so they always get given the same static IP address.
Discover and note useful information about the USB sound cards with commands :

```
lsusb
cat /proc/asound/pcm
```

```
pi@raspberrypi:~ $ cat /proc/asound/pcm
00-00: bcm2835 ALSA : bcm2835 ALSA : playback 8
00-01: bcm2835 ALSA : bcm2835 IEC958/HDMI : playback 1
01-00: USB Audio : USB Audio : playback 1 : capture 1
pi@raspberrypi:~ $
```

In the example above our USB audio device is on port plughw:1,0

77

On the receiving Pi

Open up port 8086 in your firewall with:

```
sudo /sbin/iptables -I INPUT 1 -p tcp --dport 8086 -j ACCEPT
```

and check it has been accepted with

```
sudo iptables-save
```

```
pi@raspberrypi ~ $ sudo iptables-save
# Generated by iptables-save v1.4.21 on Thu Apr 28 19:39:04 2016
*filter
:INPUT ACCEPT [3977:258407]
:FORWARD ACCEPT [0:0]
:OUTPUT ACCEPT [11006:634460]
-A INPUT -p tcp -m tcp --dport 8086 -j ACCEPT
COMMIT
# Completed on Thu Apr 28 19:39:04 2016
pi@raspberrypi ~ $
```

then set the Pi listening with

```
nc -l -p 8086 | opusdec - - | aplay -D plughw:0,0 -f dat
```

if you don't set the receiving Pi going first, the sender will fail.

```
pi@raspberrypi ~ $ nc -l -p 8086 | opusdec - - | aplay -D plughw:0,0 -f dat
Decoding to 48000 Hz (2 channels)
Encoded with libopus 1.1
ENCODER=opusenc from opus-tools 0.1.9
ENCODER_OPTIONS=--bitrate 64 --max-delay 0 --comp 0 --framesize 2.5 --hard-cbr
Playing raw data 'stdin' : Signed 16 bit Little Endian, Rate 48000 Hz, Stereo
[\] 00:01:00
```

You can force the receiving Pi to use the 3.5mm headphone output, instead of HDMI audio out, with:

```
amixer cset numid=3 1
```

On the sending Pi:

Plug in your USB Audio Mic device and use commands:

```
lsusb
```

and

```
cat /proc/asound/pcm
```

```
pi@raspberrypi:~ $ cat /proc/asound/pcm
00-00: bcm2835 ALSA : bcm2835 ALSA : playback 8
00-01: bcm2835 ALSA : bcm2835 IEC958/HDMI : playback 1
01-00: USB Audio : USB Audio : playback 1 : capture 1
pi@raspberrypi:~ $
```

The correct audio device here is plughw:1,0 - see below. The correct IP address in the example below should be the Pi you are transmitting to:

```
arecord -D plughw:1,0  -f dat | opusenc --bitrate 64 --max-delay 0 --comp 0 --framesize 2.5 --hard-cbr - - | nc 192.168.1.18 8086
```

(The command above all goes on one line)

```
pi@raspberrypi:~ $ arecord -D plughw:1,0 -f dat | opusenc --bitrate 64 --max-delay 0 --comp 0 --framesize 2.5 --hard-cbr - - | nc 192.168.1.30 8086
Recording WAVE 'stdin' : Signed 16 bit Little Endian, Rate 48000 Hz, Stereo
Encoding using libopus 1.1 (low-delay)
-----------------------------------------------------
   Input: 48kHz 2 channels
  Output: 2 channels (2 coupled)
          2.5ms packets, 64kbit/sec CBR
 Preskip: 120

[/] 00:05:37.89 0.997x realtime,    64kbit/s
```

If the command above exits immediately, then the port 8086 probably isn't open on the receiving Pi (or you haven't set the receive command running on the other Pi). Check the correct port is open on the receiving Pi with:

```
sudo iptables-save
```

Audio Mixer Panel

On the sending Pi it might be useful to play with the USB soundcard control panel using the command:

```
alsamixer
```

Press F6 and choose the USB sound card.

You can use the arrows keys to move around and raise or lower the volume levels and use M to toggle items on or off (like Auto Gain). Esc to quit.

Different audio sampling rates

At the moment we're capturing audio in stereo at 48000Hz, which is higher quality than a CD. If capturing CCTV audio and streaming it over the internet, then we can manage with a lower sample rate and single channel mono.

Either of these commands will make a local recording at a lower sample rate:

```
arecord -D plughw:1,0 -f S16_LE -c1 -r8000 -t wav test8000.wav
```

```
arecord -D plughw:1,0 -f S16_LE -c1 -r22050 -t wav test22050.wav
```

You could for example use a PIR sensor, connected to the Pi's GPIO pins, to only record audio for a set duration (-d) when motion is detected and have the filename be the date and time.

You can compare the file sizes with

```
ls -al
```

The 8000Hz sample rate generates the smallest files and is okay for speech. The 22050Hz sample rate is equivalent to FM radio. 44100Hz is CD quality and 48000Hz is DAT or DVD audio.

Try this one on the receiving Pi:
```
nc -l -p 8086 | opusdec - - | aplay -D plughw:0,0 -f S16_LE -c1 -r8000 -t wav
```

and this on the transmitting Pi:
```
arecord -D plughw:1,0 -f S16_LE -c1 -r8000 -t wav | opusenc --bitrate 64 --max-delay 0 --comp 0 --framesize 2.5 --hard-cbr - - | nc 192.168.1.8 8086
```

(commands all go on one line, type it in. Don't copy & paste from the PDF)

If you want to capture the audio into a file at the receiving end, you can do this instead:

```
nc -l -p 8086 | opusdec - - > test.wav
```

and play the recording back later with

```
aplay -f S16_LE -c1 -r8000 -t wav test.wav
```

Dropping the sample rate from 48000Hz down to 8000Hz, and mono rather than stereo, means that on an original Raspberry Pi model B or A+ the %CPU cycles used with Opus (measured with command **top**) drop from around 27% to 17%. But what advantage does using Opus give us?

We used the command **iftop** to measure network traffic on each Pi while using 48000Hz and Opus compression (151Kb a second) and without compression (10x more traffic = 1.52Mb a second). At 8000Hz Mono though it turns out it's not worth using Opus (151Kb/s v 132Kb/s none).

Pan and tilt camera controller

Pan & tilt camera bracket for Raspberry Pi.

A pan-tilt bracket controlled by two servo motors will allow you to move your Raspberry Pi camera module left/right and up/down, either from your local Desktop, or via the internet over SSH, or from a web browser.

We attached a Pan & Tilt bracket with two SG90 servos to GPIO pins 23 & 24 on a Raspberry Pi.

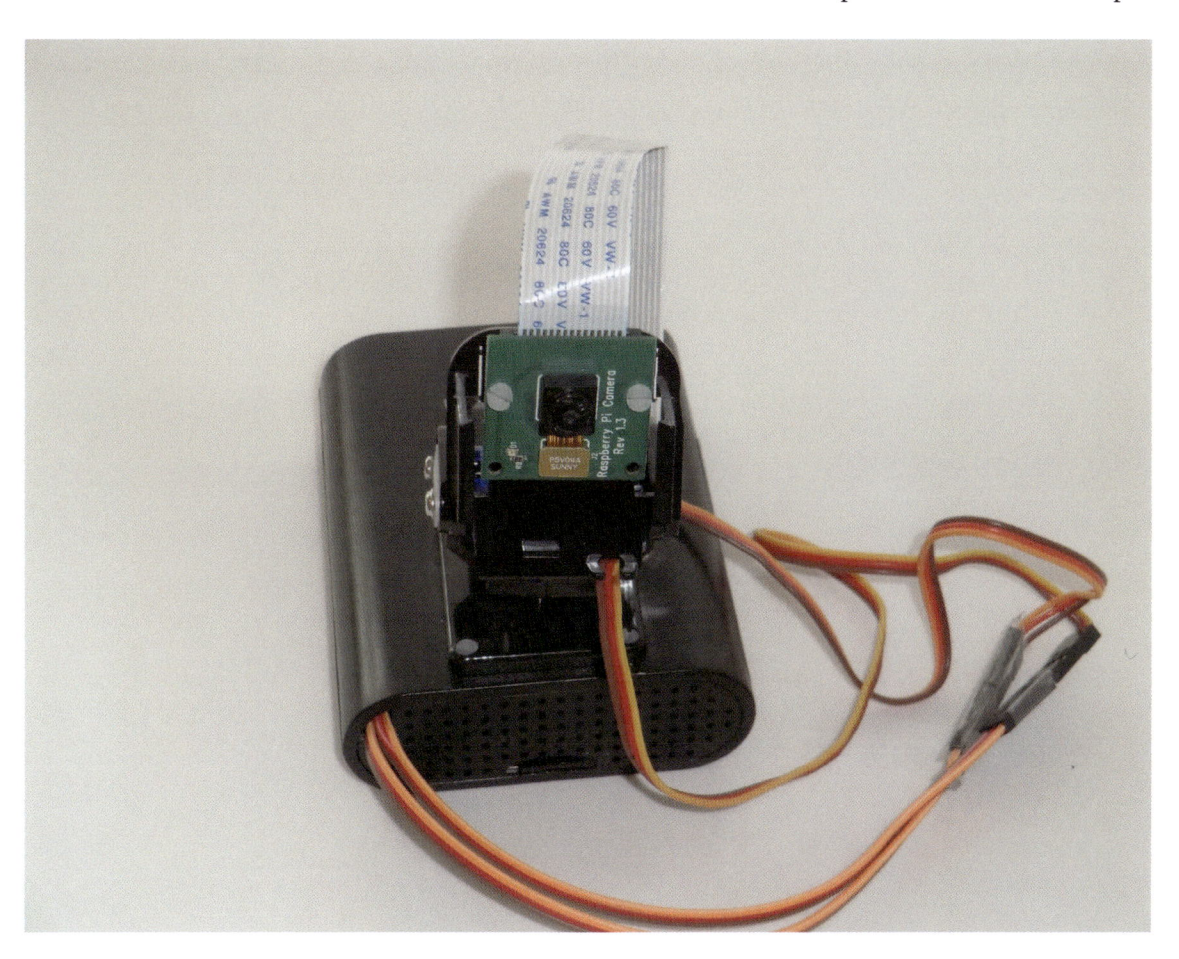

Here's a good video guide: https://www.youtube.com/watch?v=kGZxuC0i6zQ
to assembling the Pan Tilt bracket.

Wiring Diagram

Colour of wires on the servos connected to a B+ Pi.

Red = 5V+
Brown = GND
Orange = GPIO23 (Pan - left & right) or GPIO24 (Tilt - up and down)

We attached the bottom Pan servo to GPIO23 & the top Tilt servo to GPIO24 to the Raspberry Pi using some orange, red & brown male-to-female DuPont breadboard cables from eBay.

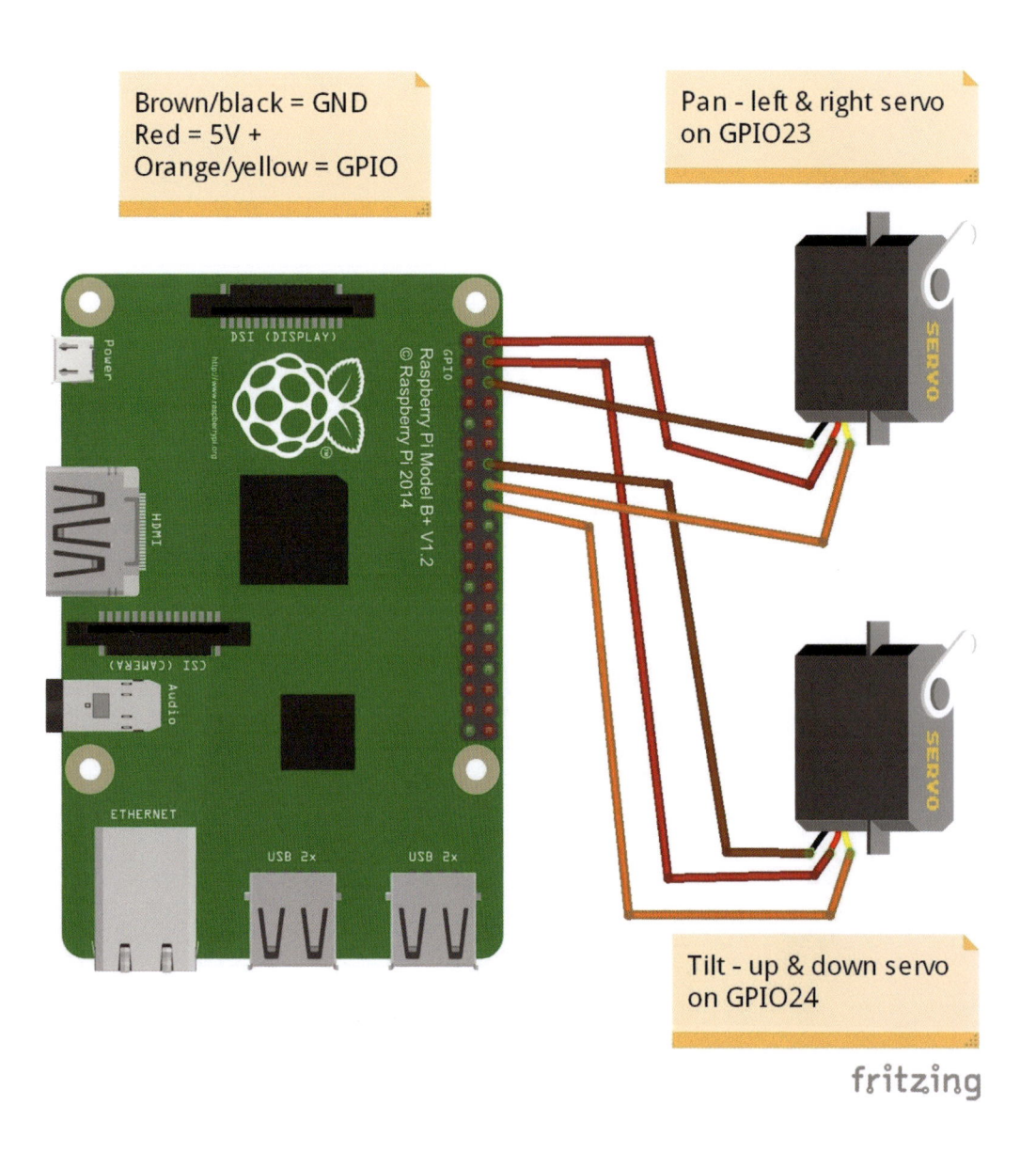

This wiring arrangement worked fine for us on older B models & newer & Pi 3 models with a 2amp USB power adapter. If the Pi reboots/freezes, then you'll need to power the Servos from batteries – see next page.

84

Use this wiring arrangement if the previous wiring diagram doesn't work reliably for you.

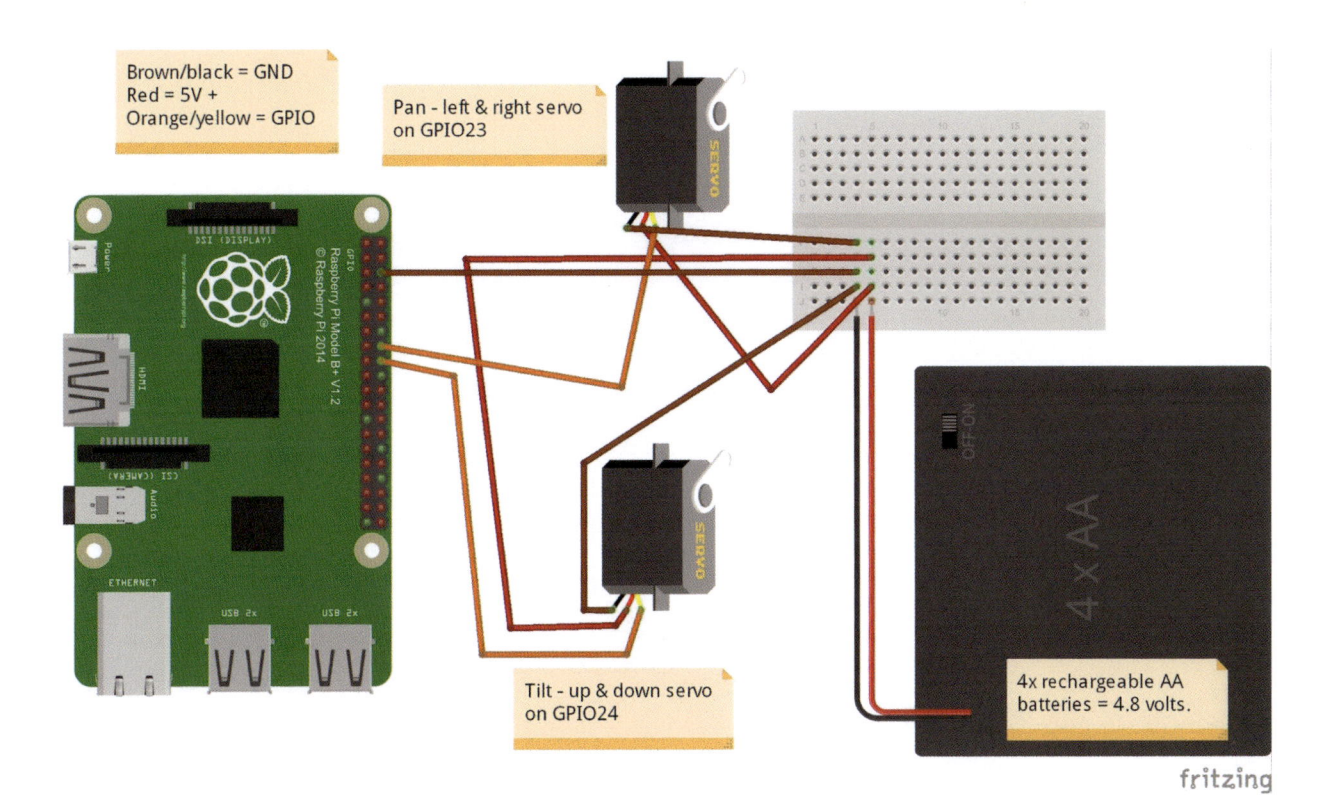

This is the more conventional way to wire servos up to a Pi, but I only discovered it after I'd already connected the SG90 servo power directly to the Pi 3 B, 2 B, B+ & A+ models, and that had worked for me without problems, 100% of the time. I've also since tested with an older model B and that also worked fine drawing 5 volts for the motors direct from the Pi. If you encounter a problem use the external battery pack method.

In the diagram above, the orange GPIO wires from the servo connect to the Pi. The brown GND cables are connected to the battery & the Pi. The red 5v+ wires from the servo are only connected to the battery. You don't have to use a breadboard, you can just tape the wires together correctly.

Servo Driver Software

We're using the open-source ServoBlaster code to control the servos from the BASH command line. We install it like this:

```
mkdir pt
cd pt
```

```
wget https://raw.githubusercontent.com/richardghirst/PiBits/master/ServoBlaster/user/servod.c
wget https://raw.githubusercontent.com/richardghirst/PiBits/master/ServoBlaster/user/Makefile
wget https://raw.githubusercontent.com/richardghirst/PiBits/master/ServoBlaster/user/init-script
wget https://raw.githubusercontent.com/richardghirst/PiBits/master/ServoBlaster/user/mailbox.c
wget https://raw.githubusercontent.com/richardghirst/PiBits/master/ServoBlaster/user/mailbox.h
```

```
make servod
sudo ./servod
```

Then test it is working with:

```
echo 5=50% > /dev/servoblaster
echo 5=10% > /dev/servoblaster
echo 5=90% > /dev/servoblaster
```

The commands above move servo number 5 (Pan left & right) on GPIO23 between centre (50%), left (10%) & right (90%) positions. The Tilt servo would be servo number 6 on GPIO24.

If you hear the servos juddering after they've stopped moving then you've moved them out of normal range. So for instance, moving servo 5 to 5% is too far for us, whereas 10% is still okay. This is why I've used 10% and 90% in my examples. You want to set the servos to 50% before assembling and fixing the pan & tilt bracket, if assembling it yourself.

You can check if servod is running with the command

```
ps ax
```

and close it with

```
sudo killall servod
```

You need to restart servod each time you restart your Pi with

```
sudo ./servod
```

You can make the servod command run each time you start your Pi by

```
sudo nano /etc/rc.local
```

Above the last line exit 0 add the line
```
sudo /home/pi/pt/servod
```

Then do Ctrl-O to save and Ctrl-X to exit & reboot your Pi, and servod should run automatically.

Desktop control panel to pan & tilt.

We've written a graphical control menu for the pan/tilt kit called ptc.py, which you run on the Pi when it's connected to a HDMI monitor, that lets you move the pan/tilt bracket around using sliders, and perform other functions too.

Also, there's a simpler command line version called ptshell.py that uses a remote SSH or local terminal to let you control the camera using the arrow keys and start or stop a video stream that you can watch using VLC Media Player on a remote Windows/Mac/Linux PC.

SSH remote pan & tilt with streaming to VLC.

Installing the web browser camera control applications.

Assuming you've just installed Servoblaster, you should still be in the pt folder. If not, `cd pt`

```
wget http://www.securipi.co.uk/pt.zip
unzip pt.zip
chmod a+x *.sh
```

Then if you're running the desktop on a Pi that's connected to a HDMI monitor.

```
python ptc.py
```

Or remotely SSH into a headless Pi and at the command line

```
python ptshell.py
```

Ptshell.py lets you move the camera around using the arrow keys and start video streaming by pressing "o". Then open VLC Media player or similar to watch the video stream.

88

Streaming video to a web browser

On your Raspberry Pi, while in the pt folder we made earlier:

`sudo apt-get install libav-tools git python3-picamera python3-ws4py`

Download the zip file with

`wget http://www.securipi.co.uk/ps.zip`

`unzip ps.zip`

`chmod a+x *.sh`

`python3 server.py`

Then go to the remote PC, open a web browser to

http://ip-address-of-your-pi:8082/

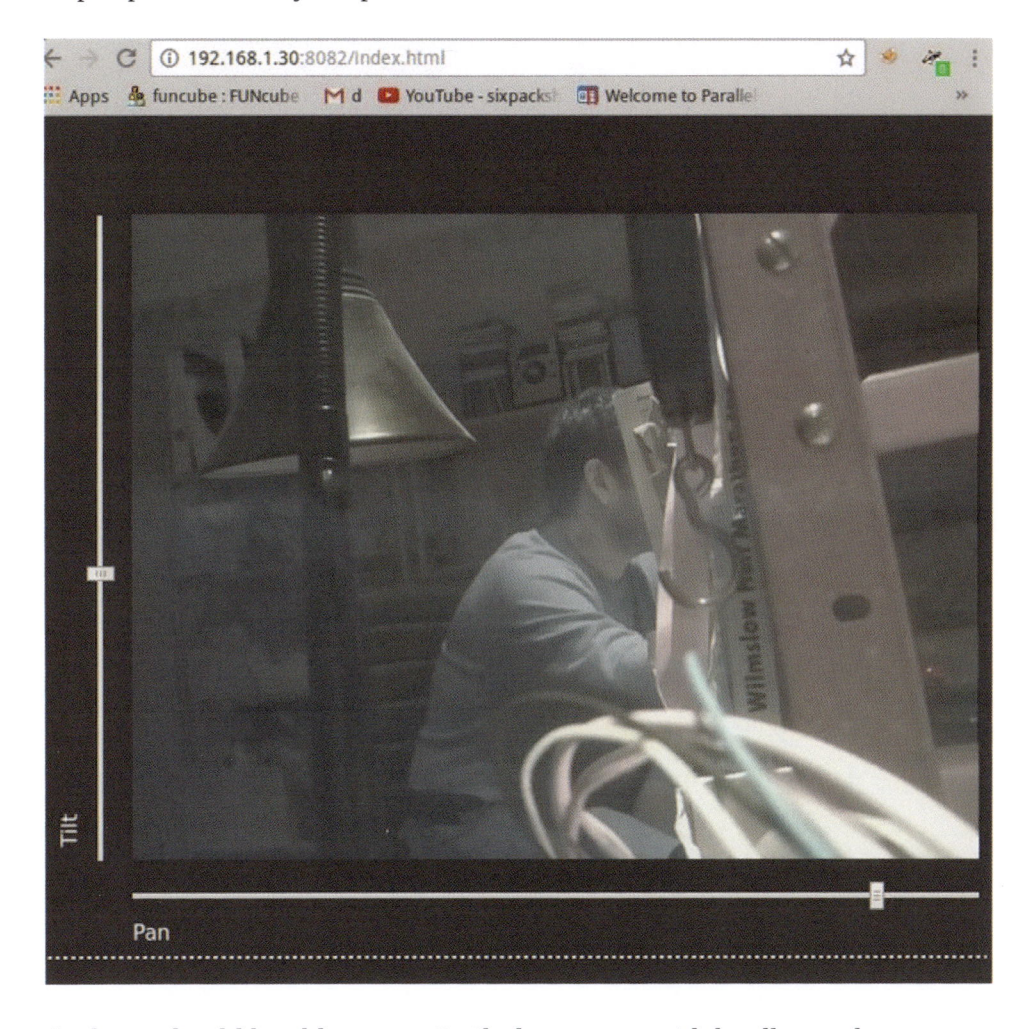

And you should be able to pan & tilt the camera with hardly any lag.

89

Printed in Great Britain
by Amazon